I AM THE NIGHT SKY

I AM THE NIGHT SKY

by the
writers and artists of
Next Wave Muslim Initiative

SAMAA ELDADAH • NOOR SALEEM • IMAAN SHANAVAS
BILAL SALEEM • SALIHAH AAKIL • LEYLA RASHEED • IMAN ILIAS
RUQAYYAH AAKIL • FATIMA RAFIE • AYAH NOOR

Next Wave Muslim Initiative /
Shout Mouse Press collaboration

Published by:
Shout Mouse Press, Inc.
1735 17th St. NW
Washington, DC 20009
www.shoutmousepress.org

ISBN: 978-1-94-543493-8

Design by Barrett Smith and Amber Colleran
Cover image, first collage © Sobia Ahmad
www.sobiaahmad.com

Author photos © Lana Wong.
All original artwork created by teen artists unless otherwise indicated. The image used on page 131 is licensed under a Creative Commons license and sourced from clipart-library.com.

For information about special discounts for bulk purchases, please contact Shout Mouse Press sales at 240-772-1545 or orders@shoutmousepress.org.

Shout Mouse Press can bring speakers to your class or event. For more information, contact Shout Mouse Press at 240-772-1545 or kathy@shoutmousepress.org.

For our younger selves
who grew up needing this book,
and for our young brothers and sisters,
who will grow up with books like this.

"Stories matter. Many stories matter.
Stories have been used to dispossess and to malign,
but stories can also be used to empower and to humanize.
Stories can break the dignity of a people,
but stories can also repair that broken dignity."

- Chimamanda Ngozi Adichie

CONTENTS

FOREWORD

When I first heard about the idea to publish an anthology created by American Muslim teens, I was overjoyed. As an author who has been trying to add authentic and affirming portrayals of Muslims to children's literature for a number of years, I knew this was something fresh, unique, and desperately needed. Finally, American Muslim youth, unheard for far too long, would have a chance to directly share their own stories, in their own voices, unfiltered.

Months later, I met the kids who would be contributing, and I knew the collection would be something extraordinary. This group of authors and artists represents some of the tremendous diversity that exists within the American Muslim community in a multitude of ways, from race and ethnicity, to sect, to types of schooling, to the number of generations lived in the U.S., to the ways they choose to approach their faith. The group includes talented poets, musicians, storytellers, essayists, photographers, and visual artists.

Yet despite the uniqueness of each contributor, all of the teens share something in common: strong pride in their Muslim identities and a desire to be seen for who they are, on their own terms. During our conversations about the goals of the collection, it became clear that the group was not interested in focusing on negative portrayals of Muslims in the media or being drawn into political battles. These kids are fiercely unapologetic about being regular teenagers, doing and feeling the things that ordinary teens do, even as they are guided by their faith. Like the stunning collage art throughout the book, their lives are a composite of elements that blend into something layered, nuanced, and beautiful.

As you read each of these insightful and entertaining pieces, you will undoubtedly be moved by their power. These writers and artists demonstrate incredible emotional maturity as they express vulnerability in the search for love and acceptance, frustrations over global events, the daily struggles of navigating life as a teen, questions about race, faith, identity, and more. You feel their fears, triumphs, goals, and dreams through poetry, short stories, a TV show pitch, vignettes, a how-to guide, and other creative approaches. Each piece, as distinct and individual as the artists, reveals our common humanity and speaks to shared values.

You hold in your hands the result of a true team effort that built new friendships, respect, and love through collaboration. Congratulations to each of the smart and fearless young authors and artists who poured their hearts into this book. I hope you're as proud of it as I am of each of you.

Hena Khan

Hena Khan is the award-winning author of picture books like *Under My Hijab* and middle grade fiction like *Amina's Voice*. Connect with her @henakhanbooks.

INTRODUCTION

Writing this book began as an opportunity: ten teenagers from Maryland tasked with representing what it means to be young, Muslim, and American. It was both daunting and a dream. We weren't entirely sure how to proceed. So we wrote about music, life, and identity, about tug of war and finding balance. Throughout this process our goal turned into something different, something new, and cohesive. It became a hope for change, a chance to positively affect a world with which we had become discontented. We realized we had been given an opportunity to show who we are because for so long nobody believed us when we told them. False narratives and demonization made us feel as if we had to defend ourselves, but we were tired of fighting, we wanted to make something of our own. So we made this, for ourselves and for our younger selves, who grew up needing this book.

When it came time to decide on a title for our collection, my fellow authors and artists didn't know how to consolidate all of who we were. It was frustrating to have to. While writing a book about how we can't be defined, we had to find a title that would somehow "define" us. We deliberated for weeks, picking and discarding titles. We struggled to find something that meant everything to all of us.

Muslim-ish? That felt corny, like a TV show that aired before bedtime. *American, Too?* That sounded defensive, as if we had not been American before. *No Single Stories?* But Chimamanda had already said that best.

Nothing was good enough, whole enough, broad enough. We needed something that told of us as one and as pieces. But we were too may things. How could we be expected to speak with just one voice?

"I decided that every time they likened this dark
to pain, fear, or evil,
I would write a poem likening it to love, joy, and life.
For I, too, am the night sky."

In the end, the title we chose came from a piece in this collection, a line that speaks to the power we all felt while writing. The power to declare who we are. To reframe and reclaim. To tell our own stories, when all you'd heard was theirs.

We know who we are. We are intelligent, athletic and energetic, funny and strange, young and alive, writers and artists. We are boundless. We do not fit in anyone's box. We are the night sky, and we wrote these stories, reflections, and reminders so that you can know us for us. Not for what they declared us to be.

This collection, like us, contains multitudes. Bilal writes about being a wannabe rock star. Imaan imagines a dystopian Underground. Samaa creates the cartoon Kabob Squad her 8-year-old self had always longed for. Ayah responds to online hate. Through poems, essays, artwork, and stories, you will see our kaleidoscope of identity, each fiercely authentic and unique.

We wrote our truths here, all in the hopes that you will remember us for who we are. We are. And we are here.

Salihah Aakil

ARE ONE OF A KIND
ARE ONE OF A KIND · 100% ORIGINAL ·

FATIMA RAFIE

Salihah Aakil

I have come to the conclusion that the night sky is my mother. I decided this after years of wondering why people fear the dark, how they could tremble at the thought of something so similar to a hug. Something so encompassing and sheltering and strong. I realized it was my duty to love this thing they call dangerous. Because if blackness can't love blackness then where does that leave me? I decided that every time they likened this dark to pain, fear, or evil, I would write a poem likening it to love, joy, and life. For I, too, am the night sky.

I) For When They Called The Night Evil

As children we sat and watched the stars all night. Jealous that they had somewhere to belong. We reached up to touch them, and in our state didn't notice how well our hands blended into the blackness of the sky. How similar our eyes looked to the moon. How brightly we could shine. As children we never searched for beauty, we effortlessly found love in everything. Now our vision isn't so clear. But we still strive for what they tell us is too far to reach. They said we'd never touch the sky and we believed them. Until we realized that we were its children and our black blends in just right. And our eyes shine so bright, the stargazers named my sister Venus and didn't even notice they loved a black girl. The way they swore they never would.

II) For When They Said The Night Should Be Feared

Those street lamps could be moons from here. Bright with night black posts blending into the background. Those street lights could be moons if they tried, beacons guiding souls to the light, but reminding that night is nothing to fear. Those street lamps could be moons from here. Smiling down at you and I, a welcoming sight to passersby, small bulbs mimicking heavenly light. Shining and kind and cold and bright, casting shadows that laugh and dance through the night. Those street lamps could be moons from here. Could be blessings dancing among the trees. Those street lamps could be moons from here, shining since long, long past years. Those street lamps are moons from where I'm standing.

III) For When They Called The Night Cruel

Tell me the story about how you fell from the sky and only survived because the night caught you in its kind embrace. My father told me about it at bedtime but I like the story better from you. Tell me about what happened afterward. How you sat alone in darkness, high above the trees, and spoke of hope to the darkest things. How strange it must have been. But that kind night sky came to love you over time and you began to glow. Glow like the sun and you had finally found a home, no more falling. Tell me, again, how you shone, white light that cut through the night, a gentle guide, a silent friend. And in the end you and the night became immortal and now we cannot help but think of you as one.

I May Be
QUIET
BUT
I Have
LOT
POWERFUL-POWERFUL-
POWERFUL-POWERFUL-

FATIMA RAFIE

ثنائية اللسان

doubletongue

Noor Saleem

on the tip
of my tongue
lay fourteen words
to mean kindness
sixteen
to show love and
ninety-nine
to describe God
while you,
had so few
that our conversations
made me
parched
because i couldn't tell you
that your words
sapped me
of the
honey on my lips
and it was
useless
to explain,
because i never
had enough
words
to make you
understand

وَاللَّهُ خَلَقَ كُلَّ دَابَّةٍ مِّن مَّاءٍ

Allah has created every [living] creature from water.
(24:45)

salt. inspiration ii

sometimes
i feel
parched,
but
i don't know
how to
drink
from your
endless
oceans

sometimes
i ache
for
waves
to crest over
me
and wash
away
everything else
so i become
a part
of you(r)
sea
-

but
sometimes
i feel
sick
of your
salt
in my veins so
i try
to cut you
out
of me

1979

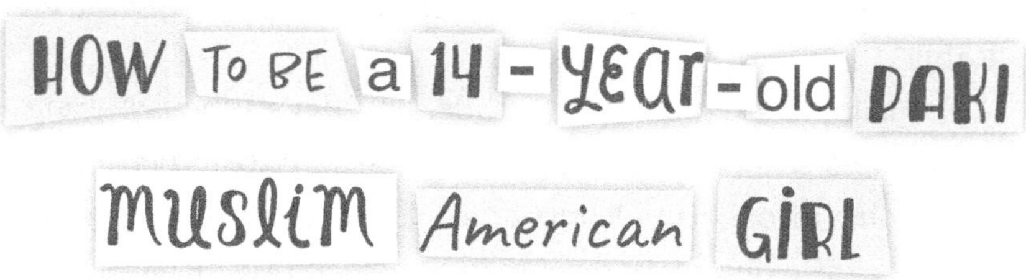

HOW TO BE a 14-YEAR-old PAKI MUSLIM American GIRL

Iman Ilias

1. Eat your green pepper, tomato, and onion omelet, Pakistani style, the way Mom makes it, the way you like it.

"Hafza, stop daydreaming, the bus will be here in five minutes!" says Baba.

It's the first day of eighth grade and he's right. The bus leaves at 7:45, and it's 7:40. I shove down the last of my omelet and turn to greet my mom before leaving.

"Acha, Mama, I'm going. Wish me luck!" I say to my mother, in the kitchen, already dressed for work. She moved to the U.S. for college twenty years ago and has no trace of her Pakistani accent left when she speaks English. My dad also came to America for college twenty-five years ago, but he occasionally mixes up his v's and w's, like "vatever" and "welocity."

"Okay, beta, have a great day," says my mother. She pulls me in for a hug.

"Allah hafiz," I say. *God be with you.* She tells me the same.

2. Meet your long-time best friend at the bus stop, wonder why she's dressed like a goth.

"Hey, what's up with the new look?" I ask as I approach Rabia.

"Hello, first day of eighth grade, first day of the last year before high school! I have to look the part," Rabia says. She's been going through an identity crisis, trying to reinvent herself since the third quarter of seventh grade when Eric Lichtenstein told her that she looked like an orangutan with long black hair.

"You don't need a new look, Rabia. What was wrong with the old one?"

"It's just that I don't want to look like one brown face in the sea of a bunch of white ones," says Rabia.

But you are brown, I think to myself. *And besides, how do boots and black eyeliner help anyway?* But I would never actually say these things to Rabia's face because I know then I'll just sound like a total mom.

3. Ride the bus, face the "Gucci Gang," try to stay strong.

Finally, the loud yellow school bus pulls up on the block. The doors hiss open and we board, Rabia first, then me.

"Howdy, girlies, how were y'all's summers? Nice to have you back on board!" exclaims our bus driver, Katie. She used to be a Southern beauty queen, but now she's a middle school bus driver. Major step down, I know, but we all adore her.

Rabia walks down the aisle and plops down a few rows behind the most irritating kids on the block, the "Gucci Gang" as I like to call them. Jackson Baker and Maria Robinson have been torturing me ever since the fifth grade.

As I walk past, Jackson says, "Hey Ugly Betty. How was your summer?"

"Better than yours," I say.

I smile as I sit down next to Rabia, thinking that was a good response. She shrugs, sighs, and looks out the window. Here we come, eighth grade.

4. Acc history class. Sort of.

The only class Rabia and I have together this year is history. My favorite subject. We're only like ten minutes in when I raise my hand and Mr. Lark calls on me.

"Mr. Lark, although what my classmate just stated is all true and based off of valid evidence, I would like to further discuss the mindset of the American people at the time when they declared independence."

I hear a groan from the corner and someone giggles. I keep going.

"Once the colonists had constructed their own economy, and become more successful on the whole, they doubted whether they needed Great Britain in their lives, dictating what they had to do. Of course, taxation without representation and the other acts of tyranny did prompt the colonists to declare independence, but it wasn't just that. It was because they knew they could be self-sufficient."

When I finish, I see some classmates rolling their eyes.

"Well," Mr. Lark says, clearing his throat, "I really enjoyed that insightful perspective, Hafza. I look forward to getting to know you this year."

I turn to smile at Rabia, but she just sinks lower in her seat, looking bored.

5. Get over it, go home, chill with your grandmothers.

"Assalamu Alaikum," I greet both my grandmothers when I walk in the door. *Peace and blessing be upon you.*

"Waalaikumsalam, meri jaan," replies my Nani, or my maternal grandmother. *And you too, my love.* My younger brother Zaid is charismatic and funny, but when it comes to my grandmothers, we all know *I'm* the favorite.

"How was school, Hafza?" asks my Dadi. (Sorry, I know it's complicated—Dadi is Urdu for 'paternal grandmother.' We basically have a different name for each and every family member!)

My grandmothers are huddled around the breakfast table, sipping chai.

"Pretty good, Dadi. What about you guys, what'd you do today?" I ask.

"Ah, the usual. Breakfast, sewing, knitting, and oh! The new episode of *Humsafar* just came out today," Nani tells me.

Humsafar is about a newly married couple who had an arranged marriage, and though they're beginning to form an understanding, those around them strongly oppose the match and try to sabotage the couple's marriage. Super corny and dramatic, I know, but it's still my favorite.

"We'll definitely watch it later," I say.

I briefly think about telling them about my day, like about Rabia and how things don't seem right between us, but I'm afraid that they'll get too worried. Besides, I'm sure it will go back to normal soon...

... or not.

6. Brush your hair, get dressed up, think positive thoughts.

By the weekend, things have not changed with Rabia. In fact, they may have gotten worse. I try not to think about this as Mama calls out to me to hurry up and get dressed. It's Pakistani dinner party time.

Mama has laid out a coral-colored kurta for me, which is like a long Pakistani tunic. It's one of my favorites. There's an intricate pattern of gold string stitched on the front and on the hems of the sleeves. I throw it on with a pair of leggings, put my hair up in a bun, and add the golden earrings that my Dadi gave me. This is how every dinner party is — we wear traditional clothes, we eat Pakistani food, and we hit repeat, like every other weekend.

This will be the first time we've had one since the start of school. In other words, the first dinner party with the "new Rabia."

"Everyone get in the car now!" Baba orders. It's also a traditional Desi bad habit to be late everywhere, so when you hear Baba asking you to come down, you know he means business.

"Yaa Khudaiya," my mom exclaims. *Oh gosh.* "Aleena's house is 45 minutes away. This will be a long drive."

No problem for me, I like long drives. I play a song in Urdu from one of my favorite Bollywood movies:

"String by string, ever so quietly,

Piece by piece, one by one,

I stitched together a dream."

Don't get me wrong, Western music is amazing, and I can listen to Pitbull any day to get me hyped, but Eastern music just puts me at ease.

And honestly, these days I need all the ease I can get.

7. Walk into the party, face the Aunties.

"Salaams, Aabidah!" Naira Aunty greets my mother. Naira Aunty has a wide smile, and is exactly like the stunning, fashionable housewives of Pakistan.

"Salaam, Naira Aunty!" I embrace her.

"Salaams, *meri jaan*," she replies. "You look so pretty, just like your mother."

My mother is adamant that before anything else, I greet all the aunties in the living room. I comply, though there are definitely certain aunties I'm not fond of. You see, there are four types of aunties:

1. The Sweet Ones, who, however much they care about their looks and the like, are still caring, and you don't mind them at all.

2. The Highbrows, who seem to critique each and every thing you do. It's impossible to ever grow to like these aunties. Steer clear of being around them, unless you've just gotten into medical school.

3. The Wise Ones, the ones who are usually older and give really good advice and have great insight. They generally never crack a smile, though.

4. Finally, inevitably, the Gossip Girls, the ones who make it their business to know everything about everyone, and who spend their time at tea parties and lunches exchanging all the latest rumors. (I heard this one aunty call one of my friends a "fast girl" who would surely bring dishonor to her family.) Do not be fooled by these aunties' inviting smiles, they're all nightmares dressed like daydreams.

Luckily I've learned the secret to pleasing all of them: always smile, don't talk too much, joke around in Urdu, and compliment their clothes. So far, so good.

8. Listen to your best friend rant about picture-perfect girls.

I run down to the basement and find Rabia sitting on the couch, browsing through her phone. She's kind of been avoiding me these past two weeks, and though part of me thinks it's because she's just stressed by all the changes (like I am!), another part of me thinks...

Well, no. I still think we'll be OK.

"Hey," I say.

She doesn't look up.

"How can Emily Perkins get her eyes to pop and her hair to be *that* silky?" she says. "And these other girls? They look like, like 14-year-old Rachel McAdams or something."

I'm confused. If Rabia wants to be a Rachel, what's with the goth? But I sense it's better just to go with it.

"You know those girls post those just to get attention," I tell her.

"They look perfect, and I look like this," she replies.

At that moment I wonder whether Rabia's goth experiment hasn't been going so well. I did hear one kid say something about 'that Indian emo' in the hallway the other day.

"Well, you're just gonna look like you, Rabia, and there's nothing wrong with that."

Rabia rolls her eyes. "Come on, Hafza."

"What? I'm just trying to help. I mean, why do you suddenly feel so bad about yourself?"

"Whatever, I'm fine," Rabia says. "And I'm not taking advice from *you*."

That one stings. But she acts like it's nothing.

"Anyways, want to get in line for food?" At Pakistani dinner parties, there's a line of dishes on the table and everyone has to literally *get in line* for food.

"Sure," I say, although I still feel hurt. And confused.

9. Grab yourself a Southeast Asian feast, chow down, get dissed. Ugh.

There's an array of foods on the table, including chicken korma (a rich curry with chicken), dum keema (beef mincemeat), and the ultimate party favorite, biryani (spicy rice!)

Rabia and I grab our dinner and then head downstairs again.

"So, how are the rest of your classes?" I ask. Since we only have history in common I want to hear about her other teachers and stuff. I love new school years.

"Fine, I guess."

That's all she says.

Suddenly another girl we know descends the stairs, and Rabia quickly gets up.

"Leena, hi!" she says to the girl. "How've you been, what's been going on?" she asks the girl, as if she's known *her* since birth, even though that's *me.*

Leena sits down next to us, but focuses all her attention on Rabia.

"Have you signed up for any clubs yet?" Leena asks. "My parents forced me to try soccer last year, but I hated it. Now I'm doing acting."

"Yeah, my parents made me join squash, but it's a drag,

so I'm gonna quit," Rabia says.

"But I thought you loved squash!" I interrupt. "You're dropping out? We've been playing together since the beginning of middle school."

"Well, yeah, I'm a new person now, Hafza. I like new things."

Rabia makes this "duh" face at Leena, and they both laugh.

"Wha...." I begin. But I don't finish. Leena just starts talking again like I don't even exist.

I remain silent for the rest of the dinner. I don't understand why my best friend of so many years can just suddenly become a different person. Now she doesn't even like the things we both used to love. What happened? She used to share everything with me, and she lived by her own rules, not anybody else's. She wasn't self-conscious all the time. The old Rabia watched Bollywood movies with me and laughed about particularly cheesy parts. She'd get her henna done with me on Eid. She was herself. Where did she go?

When Mama calls me from upstairs, telling me it's time to go home, I've never been so relieved to leave a party.

10. Think back on the things you used to share. Like Squash. And being an "All-Rounder."

Generally, I absolutely suck at sports. Even when jumping rope in first grade, I had absolutely no coordination. All the kids used to groan if they had to be on my team, and I got comments like, "How are you bad at badminton? It's like the easiest sport ever."

I consoled myself by remembering that sports weren't my

domain, school was. Those kids in P.E. may be more athletic, but I was smart, and that was good enough for me. Until one day, when my parents gave me 'the talk.' No, not *that* talk, the one about what I needed to do in order to get into the Ivy League.

"Hafza, beti, you need to excel at everything," my parents said. "These colleges, they like to see *all-rounders*, kids who do everything: studies, music, sports, and other extracurricular activities. You need to stand out on the paper, Hafza! Cello, ballet, karate, soccer, none of those were your cup of tea. Maybe let's try something new, like, squash?"

Squash, a sport whose name reminded me of someone crushing a long, weird fruit. Great, this sounded like my next big mistake.

"Sure, Mama and Baba, if I have to do it to get into Harvard, I'll do it," I said.

Plus, I knew Rabia had already joined the team. So how terrible could it be?

11. Decide you are sticking with it. Even if your teammate quits.

The answer? Pretty terrible.

For the first many months, I played horribly. Whenever I had to play a match I would get totally creamed. I mean, crème brûlée creamed. It was bad.

Finally, my family couldn't take it anymore. We couldn't bear the constant embarrassment and dejection every session brought. So we gave the manager an ultimatum: find a way to improve my skills, and fast, or we're out of here. And just like that, I was assigned a new coach: Asif *Bhai*, or 'older brother' in Urdu.

Asif Bhai was a tall, lanky man who wore a bandana around his head to keep the hair out of his eyes. He could hit a squash ball so hard it was scary. He was vicious, but hilarious. Rabia thought I was so lucky — she loved to join us for training sessions when she could. He would make us work so hard during our lessons—constantly running, doing drills, doing push-ups—but it all felt worth it afterwards. Especially since I was going through it all with my best friend. She always made me laugh, even when I literally fell on my face. She cheered me up, and helped me to believe that I really could get better. With her, even this challenge was fun.

As for squash, my relationship with it changed forever. Like the arranged marriage of Ashar and Khirad in the drama *Humsafar*, I didn't know anything about squash at first, but I learned so much about it that eventually, I fell in love with it. Squash has now taught me so much about life, like how to control my anger, how to never lose focus, and how to always hold your head up high, even when your chances of winning look terrible.

Even like, right now.

I can't believe Rabia said she's dropping out of squash. Playing on the team together used to be where we got to bond and blow off steam, and now apparently I have to go it totally alone. But—and I surprise myself here—I know I'm not going to quit, even if Rabia does. With or without her, I still love squash and I've worked hard. She may be going in a different direction, but I need to do what feels right for me.

Now the question is: Will I have to go solo both on the court AND off?

These are the things I ponder on our long drive home.

12. Get home, detox, and listen to your elders.

My Nani and Dadi are doing needlework while watching TV when I get home. I settle down to join them, hoping to get lost in the on-screen drama. After a little while my Dadi says she needs to use the restroom, so we hit pause.

"Your friend, Rabia— is everything all right between you two?" my Nani asks. I'm surprised she's noticed any tension, but I shouldn't be. My Nani notices everything, especially about me.

I take a deep breath.

"I'm confused, to be honest," I say. "Rabia and I have been best friends forever, and now, suddenly, she's all standoffish and it seems like she wants nothing to do with me."

"Do you remember doing or saying anything to make her angry?"

"I don't think so. But she's been feeling really insecure lately. She really wants to fit in and be popular, and I keep telling her that she doesn't have to change who she is for anyone."

"At your age, beta, we all feel that way. All of us want to feel like we belong. I'm glad you don't want to change yourself because that shows that you have a strong character. But you know what it's like to not fit into the crowd, right?"

She's right. Everyone sees me as this headstrong, determined girl, and yes, that is definitely a side of me. But, sometimes I do feel left out. Like at the dinner party— sometimes I feel like there's a herd, and I'm not part of it.

"I understand what you mean, but what should I do about Rabia? She was my best friend, and now, it's like I lost her," I ask.

"Jaani, that's ultimately something you have to think

about. How true a friend is Rabia to you? Are you willing to work to keep her as your best friend? If so, then you need to sit down and talk with Rabia, and tell her about how her behavior makes you feel. Friends fight, but true friends will always find a way to resolve their conflicts."

I think about what she says. She's right. If Rabia really does mean that much to me, I'll have to tell her how I really feel. We'll have to have a hard talk if we want to make everything okay again. But that's gonna take time. Lots of time.

My Dadi returns from the bathroom and we turn back to the TV. I get lost in the drama again so I can forget my own, at least for a little while.

13. Pray Isha, the night prayer. Pray for the ability to deal.

I wash my hands, mouth, nose, face, head, arms, and feet, completing the ritual of wudu, or cleansing, before prayer. Then I wipe myself dry with a towel and take out my prayer rug, crimson red with golden tassels and the image of a wide-domed mosque on it. I put on a hijab before praying, and then raise my hands to my ears.

I have always loved the night prayer. In the most fast-paced moments of life, it slows everything down. My grandmother always says, *God treasures Isha most, because you are fighting sleep to please Him*. It's a time to reflect on the day so you can make a better tomorrow.

When I pray, words of Arabic slip from my mouth, but I know them only as prayer; I don't actually know what I'm saying. In those moments, it is not about the meaning. It's about the focus. So I focus on the reasons why I'm praying, who I'm praying for. I try to remember my roots, and my purpose. I often think about my personal life, about earthly things, and tonight is no exception. But I also try to remember that there is so much more beyond our own personal experience, beyond the daily stresses and worries. I try to remember that there's a Being orchestrating everything that happens to me, and watching all that I do.

Tonight I pray for friendship. I pray that all who drift apart can find connection. I pray that everyone in need of companionship finds a friend. I pray that all who are searching for themselves can find what they seek. And in my small corner of the world, I pray that things will work out with Rabia.

I turn my head over my right shoulder, and then over my left, ending the prayer.

I AM
WHO I A
AND NO
ONE CA
CHANGE THAT

RUQAYYAH AAKIL

Name: Salihah A.

Worksheet No. 1

Fill in the Blank:

Come celebrate with me the fact that every day ________ has tried to kill me and has failed.

Something Nothing Everything

Multiple Choice:

1. When I told the teacher what happened she didn't...
   a. Know
   b. Care
   c. Both, didn't know or care
   d. Neither, didn't know nor didn't care
   e. Something in between

2. Somedays I feel I have to apologize...
   a. For my skin
   b. To my skin
   c. Not at all

3. When he called me less than human his voice became...
   a. A dagger.
   b. A bullet.
   c. A noose.
   d. My funeral.
   e. My pain.
   f. My fear.
   g. My reason to keep going.

4. This wouldn't have happened to me if I were...
   a. White
   b. Male
   c. Straight
   d. Rich
   e. Privileged
   f. American
   g. All of the above

5. I keep going because...
   a. I'm strong.
   b. I have no other choice.
   c. I want to prove them wrong.
   d. I have dreams.
   e. I have everything to live for.
   f. I can.
   g. _______ needs me.
   h. Why wouldn't I?

Essay Questions:

How do you celebrate the fact that you're still breathing?

Who named you? What have you named yourself?

If you could throw yourself a party, to celebrate simply being alive, who would you invite? Why?

EXPLORE
Math

Talk
Travel
Launch
Land
Science

KABOB SQUAD TAKES DOWN PROPAGANDA MAN

(A Concept for the TV Show I Needed as a Kid)

story by Samaa Eldadah
art by Fatima Rafie

Kabob Squad Takes Down Propaganda Man is the story of four Muslim girls taking down the infamous and dangerous Propaganda Man. It is also an ask of TV show producers to encourage representation of Muslim girls. Muslim powerhouses exist all over—organizing for social justice, dribbling on the court, styling outfits for the runway, curing diseases—challenging every stereotype. These women deserve representation in TV and film. This piece attempts to support that change.

Samaa Eldadah, 2019

-

LOG LINE:

-

Four Muslim high school girls face off against the formidable Propaganda Man, a misinformation-spreading villain who is attempting to take over the world. Styled as Powerpuff Girls meets Ms. Marvel, *Kabob Squad Takes Down Propaganda Man* would be produced as one of multiple 20-minute episodes for a teen TV channel.

Alias: Kid Genius

Strengths

Her smarts. When Plan A fails, she's got Plan B, C, and D ready to go.

Weaknesses

Social stuff. She struggles adapting to spontaneous situations.

Leena is the good girl who always has the logical solution to the problem at hand. She seems shy but when brought into conversation, will school her friends on any academic topic. Is more traditional than the rest of the team.

Alias: Moral Compass

Strengths

Her commitment to justice rarely wavers. Her moral grounding makes her invincible against Propaganda Man's misinformation.

Weaknesses

She's stubborn and sometimes unwilling to compromise, which can cause issues for the team.

Amira exudes confidence. You can feel her presence in a room. She is great at managing the team and acts as its spokesperson in communications with Justice Central.

IMAN

Alias: Speed Demon

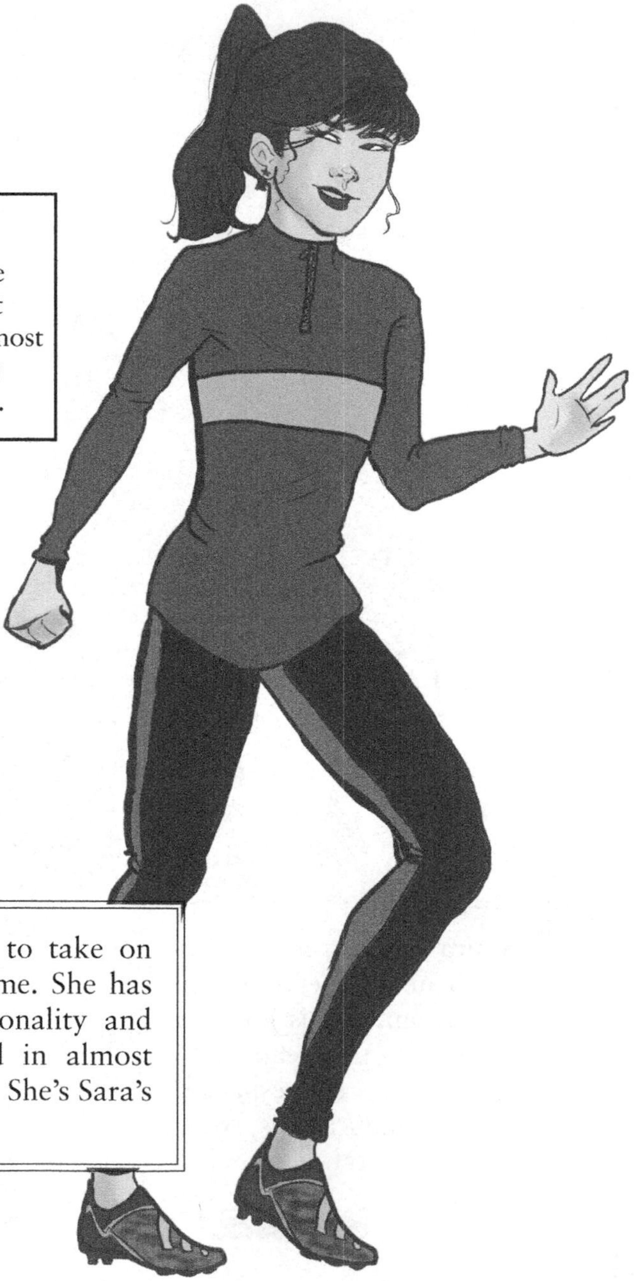

Strengths

Her super speed! She plays every sport but likes running track most of all. She's the most athletic of the group.

Weaknesses

Acts on impulse. Her instinct and gut reactions can get her in trouble.

Iman is ready to take on anything anytime. She has a bouncy personality and finds the good in almost every situation. She's Sara's twin.

Alias: Muscle Machine

Strengths

Literal strength! She trains daily at her gym and has quads of steel.

Weaknesses

Like Iman, she's impulsive. She'd rather just go for it than develop a plan.

Sara is a weightlifter. Not only does she have major physical strength but also takes a lot on for the team.

PROPAGANDA MAN

Strengths
Highly manipulative. Can talk to people and convince them of his worldview without them realizing they've been hypnotized. He maintains a grip on Citizens residents through hacking screens City-wide and broadcasting videos of himself talking to the people, i.e. those he convinces to do his bidding.

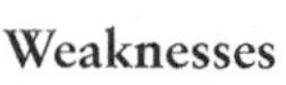

Weaknesses
Because he continuously broadcasts his own image, his real identity can be exposed to viewers.

Propaganda Man is an evil hacker who manipulates people through internet misinformation. He most recently has dressed up as City Mayor, convincing the City that he is their new leader.

City Mayor

@realcitymayor

Committed to your security and well-being.

Who to follow

City Security Forces
@citysecurity

City Mayor Videos
@cityvids

City News
@citynews

Outsider Invasion Watch
@invadercam

Trends for you

#keepthemout
#outsiderinvasion
#citymayor
#securitythreat

City Mayor
@realcitymayor
ALERT: Our borders have been overwhelmed with waves of Outsiders. Our brave forces have been dealing with the crisis. Be on the lookout!
10:35 AM · 15 Feb 18 · Twitter For Android
4,504 Retweets 17K Likes
City Mayor
@realcitymayor
Let's be real: Outsiders are illegally coming onto OUR land, causing disruptions and threats to our well being. We CANNOT allow this to continue.
3:02 PM · 13 Feb 18 · Twitter For Android
5447 Retweets 18K Likes
City Mayor
@realcitymayor
We should be DONE with political correctness by now. Let's prioritize the security of all Citizens and call these threats what they really are!
2:55 PM · 13 Feb 18 · Twitter For Android
6002 Retweets 16K Likes

City Mayor
@realcitymayor

Citizens! Due to health issues, our former mayor has stepped down. I will be taking her place. Tune in here. THE WORK BEGINS!

Voiceover Guy:

Amidst the pressures of being that one Muslim in school, that token on the diversity promo, that dictionary for all Islam/Arab/terrorist/ Middle East-related questioning, four girls came together to form the most powerful girl syndicate in the history of the City.

They work for justice under the guise of regular shmegular Muslim girls, but around the City they were known as Kabob Squad– powerhouse Muslimas and legends of their time.

We now find our heroes on another mission to save the world...

[Musical Intro]

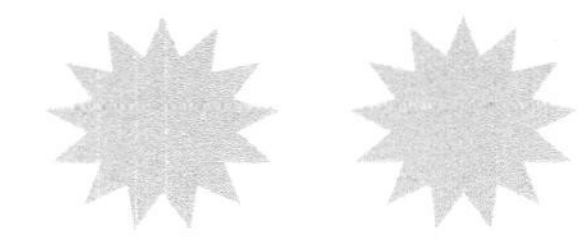

EP 1

The girls have just heard the latest update from Justice Central: Propaganda Man has struck again with a new and dangerous misinformation campaign and is posing as the new City Mayor! He has hijacked access to screens across the City and is using manipulation to hypnotize Citizens. It looks like our favorite four are back in business. Will their strengths match up against Propaganda Man's newfound power?

INT. BASE - DAY

Girls are at base, a high-tech covert facility conveniently hidden behind the local kabob shop in East City. Amira is powering up a projector in the background, Sara and Iman are comparing notes on their latest athletic achievements, Leena is fuming and looking at her watch.

SARA:

Iman, first of all do you see this level of muscle? I've been on a new protein regimen.

LEENA:

Guys! What's up? Aren't we here for a mission? I got the Justice Central alert, I assume we're here to get stuff done, right? I need to study for Calculus so this best not be a false alarm...

AMIRA:

Yeah, this is real. I'm gonna pull up Sofia. Justice Central has news for us.

IMAN:

Sara, do you understand how good these pants are? So BREATHABLE. These babies are gonna be my best friend in preseason.

LEENA:

Nice that you guys are geeking out but...

IMAN:

Lol, says the geek...

Sara and Iman laugh, good humoredly. Amira finally pulls the stuff up on the screen. Everyone falls silent as they see their mentor's face.

SOFIA:

Hey ladies, we don't have much time so I'm gonna cut right to the chase. Our receptors have been picking up major vilification of Outsiders and use of manipulation to rile up hate. This is VERY characteristic of Propaganda Man. Do you remember we talked briefly about him when we discussed this year's villain list at orientation? He's the latest threat and you all are the closest team to him. Justice Central is asking you to take him down and neutralize him. Justice Central believes in you and I do too. Don't doubt your capabilities. Good luck, Kabob Squad.

Sofia signs off, girls are left silent in front of a black screen.

LEENA:

WHAT? You guys, this is no joke. If we make a mistake we're going to jeopardize the planet.

AMIRA:

I don't think so. She seemed really serious when she sent me the data on PM.

LEENA:

I calculate that we have a 98.4% chance of dying...

IMAN:

YOU GUYS. Are you kidding me? This is the opportunity

of a lifetime! We go in, take him down, get recognition from all of Justice Central in their time of need and basically save the world! What's not to be excited about?

SARA:

I agree. You guys, there's obviously gonna be danger. But that's why we do what we do! Who says we're not able to take this on?

AMIRA:

Justice Central is counting on us.

LEENA:

Ok, maybe there's a 93.2% chance...

AMIRA:

We don't have time to debate this. We got the assignment, so let's get to it.

Screen comes back to life, this time with Propaganda Man's mug shot staring out into the distance. Leena takes the lead, pointing her laser at an analysis of Propaganda Man's strengths and weaknesses. The rest of the team is around the table paying attention.

LEENA:

Ok you guys, here's the data. Justice Central receptors have been picking up on his activities on the outskirts of East City. His strength is hypnotizing people through videos on their screens but always from remote locations. He can access anything: TVs, phones, computers... You name it, he can hack it. All he needs is a connection to a main data network and he can blast videos to an entire geographic location. Last time Justice Central caught him at the heart of a movement to banish the Outsiders. It says here he was broadcasting fake news — essentially a fear campaign about them taking over City land. It takes one minute of watching him for you to be hypnotized and an hour for the effects to wear off.

EXT. CITY STREET - DAY

Iman and Sara run down a City street. Iman looks at location-hologram-pinging-device on her wrist.

IMAN:

Just got the location data from Leena.

SARA:

Ok, let's do this. Is your earpiece on?

IMAN:

Yeah, let's go.

SARA:

Ok wait. We need to make sure no one mistakes us for Outsiders though. Who knows what people who've already been hypnotized would do.

IMAN:

Good point. Let's do this.

Montage of the girls running through the City, jumping over barriers, and hiding behind buildings to evade hypnotized Citizens. After a few moments, they stop outside Propaganda Man's hideout, a sinister, dark industrial building.

IMAN (WHISPERS):
Ok, once we get inside, I'll find out how to get the camera on so the people can see him for who he really is.

SARA:
I'm sure he'll have a remote or something. But be careful. We can't get hypnotized ourselves. If you need to, close your eyes and ears.

IMAN:
I got this, don't worry. I'll let you know once I've turned the camera on and he's said enough.

SARA:
Ok great. I'll get in from the back to turn the electricity off so he can't spin a new story.

IMAN:
Awesome. Can you get me in through a duct or something?

SARA:
Yeah. I'll meet you out here when you're done, ok?

IMAN:
Sounds like a plan!

Sara hoists open a metal door to a duct on the outside of the building. Iman slips inside.

INT - PROPAGANDA MAN'S STUDIO - DAY

Iman has reached Propaganda Man's makeshift studio in his basement through the ducts. She peers out from behind the vent, watching Propaganda Man. A projection of the real Mayor's office glows on a screen behind him as he finishes his latest broadcast to the Citizens.

PROPAGANDA MAN:

That, fellow Citizens, is why we must be on the lookout for Outsiders. You never know what they could do next! We must protect our City from harm!

Propaganda Man ends the broadcast with a remote that he leaves on the table. Iman eyes the remote, wondering how she can get to it.

IMAN:

How am I supposed to get to that and expose him for everyone to see?

Propaganda Man's walkie-talkie crackles across the room. He walks over to receive the message. As he walks over, Iman darts out of the duct, grabs the remote, and gets back in the duct, closing the vent behind her.

HENCHMAN 1 (OVER WALKIE-TALKIE):

Mr. Mayor! There's a Outsider out back causing a disturbance! We will ensure she's taken care of.

PROPAGANDA MAN:

Hahaha! Another Outsider down! Make sure she doesn't get away.

IMAN (WHISPERS TO SARA):
Sara, are you the disturbance this Henchman is talking about? I have the remote and the camera's on now! I'm gonna come as soon as I can but I need to do this first.

SARA (WHISPERS BACK):
Ok come quickly. I can't fend them off for too much longer.

Propaganda Man laughs to himself, celebrating his success at taking over the City, unaware that Iman has turned the video camera back on. He's LIVE to the whole City.

PROPAGANDA MAN:
I've really gotten the City this time. They'll believe ANYTHING I say. Hah, Justice Central thought they could catch me. Now I have everyone under my command.

Propaganda Man looks up and sees that the green blinking light indicating "Live Broadcast" is on. He backtracks, looking startled. Sweat drips down his face.

PROPAGANDA MAN:
Uhhhh, ha ha. I was just repeating something the Outsiders say! They are always trying to, uh, take control of our City! Right, Citizens?

Screens go black across the City. Network access is temporarily disabled.

LEENA (OVER EARPIECE):
Girls! I heard you say Sara was in trouble so I figured out how to overcome their internet security and blast through

the firewalls with a special code from Justice Central. I pretty much disabled his electricity remotely!

Screen is still black, but you can hear sounds of scuffle. When lights go back on, we see all of Kabob Squad surrounding Propaganda Man. Amira is wrestling him into handcuffs.

PROPAGANDA MAN (SPLUTTERS):
What! How are you not hypnotized? Where are my henchmen? How did my plan get foiled by YOU fools?

AMIRA:
First of all, let's get you silenced.

She wraps a bandana around his mouth.

LEENA:
Second of all, for a hacker, you have a pretty unsecure system. I was able to take down your electricity on my way over here from my own phone, dude.

SARA:
Third of all, your henchmen were no match for my toned muscles. I got on a new protein regimen and it's been—

AMIRA (HISSES):
Sara!

SARA:
What? You're not here for my whey protein lifestyle?

IMAN (INTERJECTS):
Fourth of all, you were the one who exposed yourself. All I needed to do was push a button.

AMIRA:
In the name of justice, you're hereby done with villainy forever, Propaganda Man. Your reign of fear is over!

Amira handcuffs Propaganda Man, who squirms and then slumps in his chair. A Justice Central agent has just arrived and stands in the open doorway.

JUSTICE CENTRAL AGENT:
We'll take him from here, ladies. We'll keep in touch.

IMAN:
YEEEEEEEHAWWWWW. That's what I'm TALKING ABOUT!

Voiceover Guy:

With their mission complete and justice restored to the City, the girls are ready to take a long deserved break. They know, however, that the fight for justice will continue. In Episode 2, the ferocious four are up against their most dangerous enemy to date, Superstruct. Can they break down his walls? Find out, Mondays at 8:00, only on Snicktoon.

[Musical Outro]

~ WOMAN ~
I
Wear

Shall
~MUSLIM~
Today?

Standing Out

Ayah Noor

I stand out a lot.

When I was younger the only thing that stood out about me was how tall I was compared to everyone else.

I remember going to pools and parks and playgrounds with my friends and other kids my age looking years older than I was. I didn't have the "spunky sarcasm" I have now. I didn't "embrace" anything. I was an awkward, shy, gorgeous little girl who lived in a world of her own.

Now I wear a hijab.

When I walk around no one has to play a guessing game. They know what I am even though they don't know who I am.

I love wearing a hijab. I love the meaning and purpose behind it. But there are times when it feels lighter or heavier on my head.

There are times when I don't even remember I have it on, until a random gust of wind blows in my face and ruins hours of styling and drapery effects.

There are other times when I can feel every thread of it being burnt to a crisp by hundreds of eyes.

I don't care. I shouldn't care. So why do I?

Why should I have to worry about how I project myself to the world? Why should I worry if someone is going to randomly insult me?

Some people might tell me not to worry. Those same people are often ordinary white Americans who can walk in wherever they want to without thinking twice, who can go places without googling whether or not the area likes "their type of people," who can just go about their day not having to worry.

But honestly, why are our realities so different?

Has society really made a sixth-generation American think she isn't American enough, just because of a piece of fabric?

I still stand out a lot.

These days it's because I am busy thinking about prayer and personalities and the Pythagorean theorem, still awkward, still a bit shy. But I've learned that every obstacle is there either for you to improve it, or to learn from it.

And while it sometimes takes guts, there is nothing wrong with standing out.

"Muslim men are oppressive"
"Cover your hair it's inappropriate"
"Muslim men are Savage"
"Women shouldn't be allowed to walk the streets Alone"
"ALL muslim men disrespect and degrade ALL women"
"Women shouldn't DRIVE"
"The Arab culture is PRIMAL"
"Women shouldn't hold positions of POWER"
"All Muslim men are PIGS"

FATIMA RAFIE

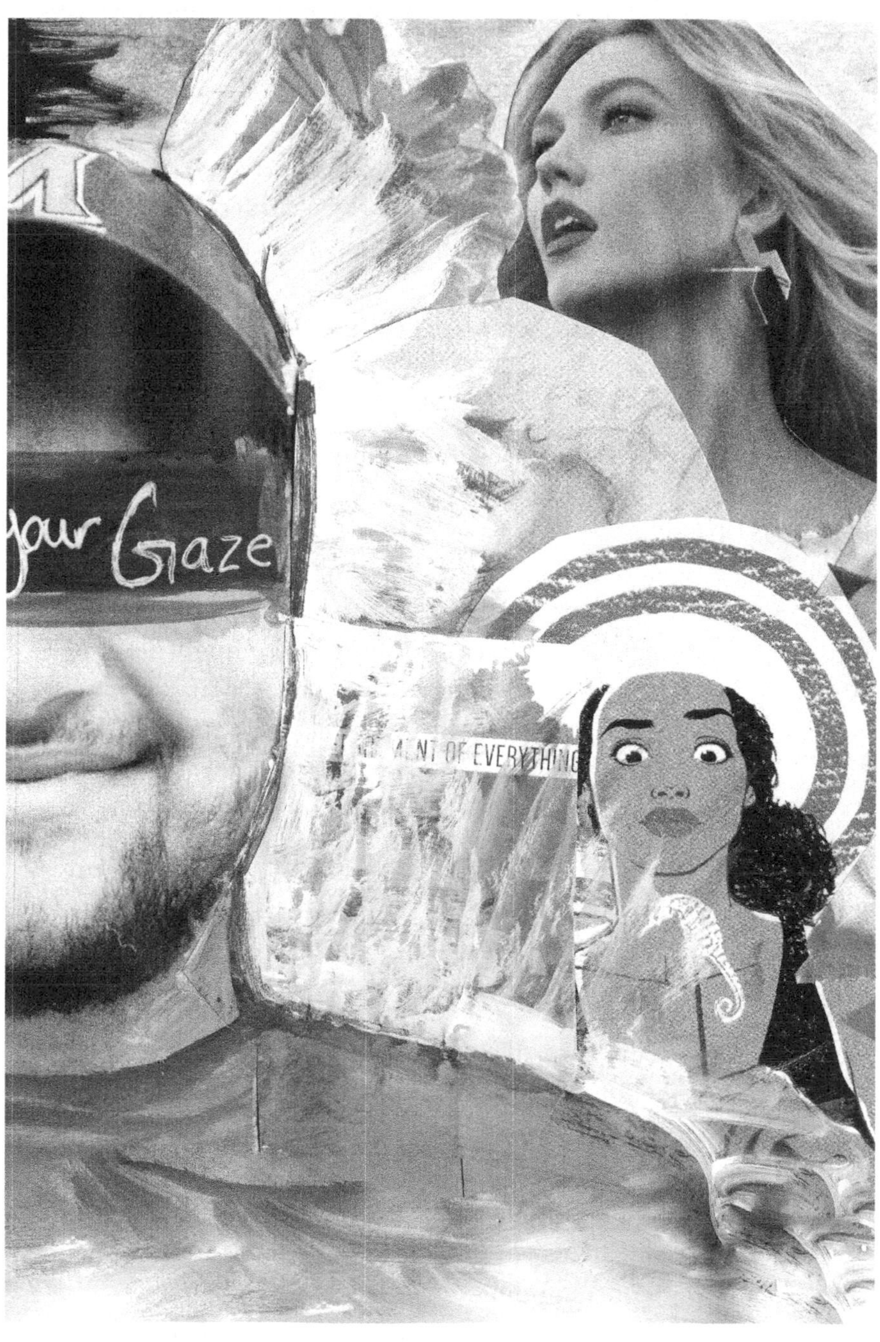

before

I used to love Friday nights. Love them almost as much as I loved my bike. Love them because those were the nights Grandma would turn her radio all the way up, open her bedroom door wide, and call us to come join her in dancing. Every Friday was a party. Me and my siblings learned freedom the best way my grandma knew how to teach us.

It was always hot when we danced. The summer nights reminded Grandma of her home in Georgia, a place where her freedom had never come easily and she had to dance to learn it, and then relearn it every time a ghost called her the n-word in passing.

One summer the A/C in our house broke—although my mom says now that she might have just turned it off because we couldn't afford it, she can't remember. But me and my family still danced. Some Muslims say music is haram, but us black Muslims can't afford to amputate that part of our heritage, can't forget what signaled our first taste of freedom.

So we danced, with our Christian grandma, and most Fridays she was drunk but we didn't know. We didn't care. She taught us love to the sound of Aretha and chirping crickets and frogs, under the moon, in a place where wings were more than the stuff of daydreams. And in the morning we would wake to Grandma's oatmeal and raisins and she would watch us pray with a pride that only comes from understanding.

I used to love Friday nights. Love them almost as much as I loved my bike, but then my bike got stolen. My only consolation was the thought that another child might be enjoying it and my grandma would probably buy me another if I asked, but it had to be on a night she was happy. Maybe a Friday.

There were still things I had to get used to in the new house — a busy street that made playing a danger, now a scarf on my head as a symbol of my pride — but I couldn't see the stars, I said I couldn't see the stars. For the first time in my life. And I heard sirens every night, spent time wondering if those were really gunshots.

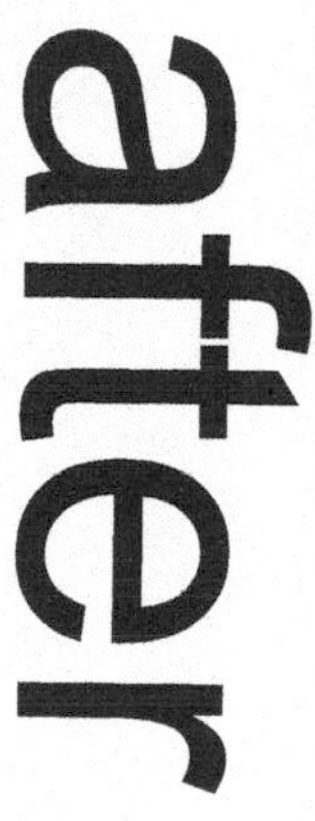

I remember one day there was a fight on my block, two men, who might have been angry about parking. One had a bat and the other a crowbar. They actually hit each other, they actually broke the windows in one another's cars. I heard the sound of bat on bone and a human being shattered. I cried that day, and prayed for both men that night.

I learned prayer and how it kinda felt like music. And I baked pineapple upside-down cakes for family birthdays and the A/C broke again, this time really broke. I laughed at memory, but learned that some things warranted tears and prayer.

But actually eight years is the longest I've ever lived in one home so this is my home, no matter how dusty and concrete. Most days I wake up grumpy with the sun in my eyes, but today I woke up singing.

FrIEnDS
moviES
FOOD
VIDEO GAMES
fAMIly
PLAYING
MUSiC

RUQAYYAH AAKIL

MUSLIM **MUSIC** THEORY 101

Bilal Saleem

(1) CONDUCTOR: (*noun*) the director. indicates the tempo, rhythm, and dynamics. responsible for unifying the performers.

It was a rager—probably over a hundred people—and happening in the middle of the damn afternoon. Ramadan was about to start, like in the next few days, so it was probably the last party I'd go to during the day until it ended. My friends and I were geeked, watching all the chaos. One dude passed out, so Trey and Alex decided to see how many french fries they could fit in his nose before he woke up. People were seriously tripping. The whole basement smelled like alcohol and smoke.

There was no way anyone else in the room would remember what happened after the party ended. Me, though—I was chilling with my water, staying hydrated. My job was to keep the music bumping, with my phone in the AUX. I was honored. My friend Diana, the host, put me in charge because "no one else can hear the harmonies like you." I don't know what it is, I can just hear the ends of different tracks coming together. The melody of one song perfectly complementing the bassline of another. Common temporal rhythms between pieces resonate in my mind. I have a reputation—whenever I'm driving with friends, or at a party, or at a kickback, or listening by myself, people generally jam to what I put on, because I guess I just hear what sounds nice. So it's almost like my duty now.

"Hey man, why aren't you getting *lit*?" some dude asked, holding a red cup.

There are a lot of things I could've said: *Because I'm a Muslim. Because I want a clear head. Because I'd rather keep my inhibitions.*

But it was booming and bumping and everything in between, plus, dude would never remember what I was gonna say anyway, so I was just like, "Deadass, I'm just tryna wake up tomorrow."

And we left it at that.

(2) INTERLUDE: (*noun*) a short piece of instrumental music that contrasts with what happens before or after.

I turned on the amp, plugged in my guitar, and felt the electric buzz run through the cord, upwards through the pickups, and into my fingers. Sparks flew between my fingertips. It was the first time I had picked it up in almost two weeks, but it still felt like home. A place where I can freely express myself, through gentle chords or raucous and shredding solos. Where I have no worries, no fear. Where I am freed from real life's nonsense, like fake friends, school deadlines, and all that other white noise. My guitar would never abandon me, or tell me lies, or deceive me, or put me down, or hurt me. Instead, it offers me a doorway into a world. A realm where your looks, your class, your ethnicity, your religion, your education, and your beliefs are all put on hold. All that matters is the sound.

I strummed a chord, and the room swelled, filling with millions of invisible waves, bouncing off the walls, diving into the floorboards. They tied together to tether me to the Earth as I prepared to spacewalk. My guitar pulled me past other planets, one note at a time, as I floated by neighboring astronauts, trading skills and pieces of music. I visited heroes to learn from them: Bowie, Page, Hendrix. Back on earth, every harmony was trapped within the room, redirecting straight into my body, resonating in my bones, warming my soul. Time stopped, and as I drifted deeper into the Milky Way, the more stars I could see.

"Mom said you have to take me to basketball practice," my brother said, yanking the tether and pulling me back to real life.

"I was in the zone, jeez. All right, get your shoes on, let's go," I said. I ruffled his hair, suddenly feeling the weight of gravity again.

I put my guitar back on its stand, and turned off the amp. The buzzing crickets faded away and echoed into its chamber, like a last-ditch effort to stop me from leaving. I put my pick down on the table instead of in the jar; I'd be back in a few.

(3) DISSONANCE: (*noun*) a lack of harmony. incompletion of chords that induces tension, or a feeling that something is missing.

The concert was supposed to start at 8:30, almost sundown, which is when I'd (finally) break fast.

The security dudes told everyone to take everything out of their pockets, and then they waved around the metal detector wand. Zack went in first, and I was following him when one of the dudes stopped me. He told me I couldn't take in the granola bar I had in my hand. They had a very strict "no outside food or drink" policy, but I couldn't bear to go through an entire concert without a bite to eat. It'd been fourteen hours since sunrise, since I had last eaten.

"Ay homes, you can't bring food in," he said as he blocked my entrance to the door and held up a trash can.

"Look, it's Ramadan, and I've been fasting all day. Y'all don't want me to pass out, right?" I looked at him straight in the eyes.

"I don't have time for this. Go speak to that man over there."

I was getting fed up, I didn't have time for it either. I had to get inside to get good spots. It would've been one thing if I were trying to hide it, or take in something like an unwrapped brownie, but it was a sealed granola bar. I knew if I got mad there was no way in hell I'd be able to bring anything in, though. I went up to the guy, who turned out to be the head of their team. He ushered me into his office.

"Dude, if I let you bring it in, then I gotta let everyone bring stuff in," he told me.

"All right, I understand that, but I won't make it a big deal to anyone else. It's been a long day, I'm fasting, and I haven't had anything since dawn, you feel me?" I said.

He looked at me for a good thirty seconds before replying. *Had he ever fasted? Did he even know what fasting was? Did he know any Muslims? Was he going to send me home?*

"Fine. But do not make it known as you exit my office. You hide all of that, and I don't care, you gotta act as if I made you get rid of it."

"Word. Thanks."

I had to deal with stuff like this all the time. Just sharp little reminders that my identity and society don't always sync up. It sucks, but whatever, it was over, and I just was happy nothing worse happened.

It was a struggle to weave my way through the crowd to get back to my friends. I somehow managed to find Zack again despite the masses of people slamming into each other just for fun. It was a mosh pit. It was great though. Every time the 808 kicked in I could feel it in my chest, every time a snare knocked it would span through both my ears, every time the crashes crashed you could see a surge of light on the stage, and plumes of steam spurting out of the sides.

My lips curled up in a smile as I pulled the half-broken granola bar out of my pocket.

"About time," I thought.

(4) MODULATE: (*verb*) to shift between two keys. to subtly blend between scales and modes and give music life and character.

"Faz! Eid Mubarak, B." I walked up to Faisal, who'd gone by Faz since the third grade.

"Let's get it, Khair Mubarak!" he replied. He laughed and gave me the traditional three hugs.

"Where's Raza? I just saw him in the *masjid*."

"I have no clue, honestly. I think his mom grabbed him to meet with relatives who he probably doesn't even remember," Faz said. He looked at my fit. "Hey, fresh *shalwar kameez*, man."

"Thanks, I got the matching 1's too." I pointed to my sneakers and smiled. "When are we headed to your place? It wouldn't be Eid if your pops wasn't making *pakoras*."

"You're hip. Let's go now, I got the car."

"I got AUX."

Faz's car was souped up to the max. He dropped his entire paycheck on a new exhaust system, twelve inch subs, a coat of red paint (our favorite color), and tinted, iridescent windows. His car was the best for listening to music in; every kick would make his headlights flicker and his mirrors vibrate.

"Nah, there's no way Beyonce is better than Rihanna," Faz said with a concerned look.

"Why are you so pressed?" I started cracking up.

"Rihanna actually has so much more talent. Only reason people say Beyonce is better is because she's got this 'Queen Bey' ego, and people think she's hotter."

"Whatever. I mess with both of them. I don't even get why people gotta compare them in the first place. You're just a hater."

"Whatever, dummy, you really wanna be blasting A$AP as we pull up to your place?"

"Oh, yeah, my parents would slap the lights out of me if they heard all that today."

"Hai hai, Faz, *bachay*, embarrassing us with all of

profanity in front of guests, huh?" I tried to keep a straight face as I did my best Desi accent.

"Shut up, fool," Faz said, cracking a smile. "Don't forget your *salaams* when you see my grandparents."

"Do I ever? Let's go."

I laughed, making a break for the door, taking off my shades, fixing my hair, and playing a different scale.

(5) CONSONANCE: (*noun*) notes that are harmonious, simply due to their place in the audible spectrum.

Usually when my grandmother drove over to our house, I'd play her in Monopoly, or she'd attempt to show me how to cook, or she'd flame my little brother and tell him to get rid of his moppy hair, but this time was different. She wanted to hear me play guitar for her. I was surprised. She had never asked before, but now after all these years she requested a song. I wondered if it had to do with the end of Ramadan. Some people are a bit more strict, not wanting to listen to music when they could be doing something more pious, especially in the last ten days of Ramadan, which are considered the holiest.

"Why did you ask today?" I asked her.

"Why do you think? I had to wait for you to be good enough. I'm the best audience you'll ever play for."

"Hm. True." I smiled and shook my head.

I thought about how I'd been playing since I was six, yet she still hadn't heard much. I mean she'd hear me noodle around or something, but never *really* play anything polished. Not anything that I felt I could show off. I thought about that one time I got to play for my grandfather before he passed away. "Over the Hills and Far Away," by Led Zeppelin. I remember the expression on his face, the pride in his eyes the moment after I struck that last chord. It was so quiet for a second that you could hear my quivering fingers drumming against the neck.

I was honored that she wanted to hear me.

I was also relieved that she didn't denounce music. Every time she'd come over I'd have my guitar sitting on display, but she had never acknowledged it—unlike every other person ever who saw it. Sometimes I'd meet an ultra-conservative-music-is-*haram* kind of person, at some wedding or gathering, and become worried that people that I cared about might end up attacking music as well. I couldn't have been more happy that my grandma wasn't one of those haters. She just wanted some quality, which I understood. If I were her, I wouldn't want to hear some buzzy, out-of-tune, scratchy, boring chords.

I was also happy that I didn't have to play Monopoly for the trillionth time.

"Okay, Naano, what do you want me to play?" I asked.

"*Mujhe nahi pata*. Something with guitar in it," she said as she looked at my brother and laughed.

"You'll like this one." I smiled.

I strummed the intro for "More Than Words," by Extreme, and immediately saw her cheeks flush. She leaned in, closed her eyes, and took a deep breath. Together we escaped into the harmony.

GLOSSARY:

BACHAY: *(singular and plural) (noun)* kid, boy. used sarcastically by *bachay* themselves to tease old folks.

MASJID: *(noun)* Arabic word for mosque.

MUJHE NAHI PATA: "I don't know."

PAKORA: *(noun)* fried dough made out of chickpea flour, onions, cilantro, and some other stuff, probably a fine layer of crack, because they're the best thing you'll ever eat.

SALAAMS: *(noun)* shortened version of the Muslim greeting, *A'Salaamwa'alaikum.*

SHALWAR KAMEEZ: *(noun)* the baggiest of baggy pants *(shalwar)* with a long dress-like tunic *(kameez)* worn in any color imaginable.

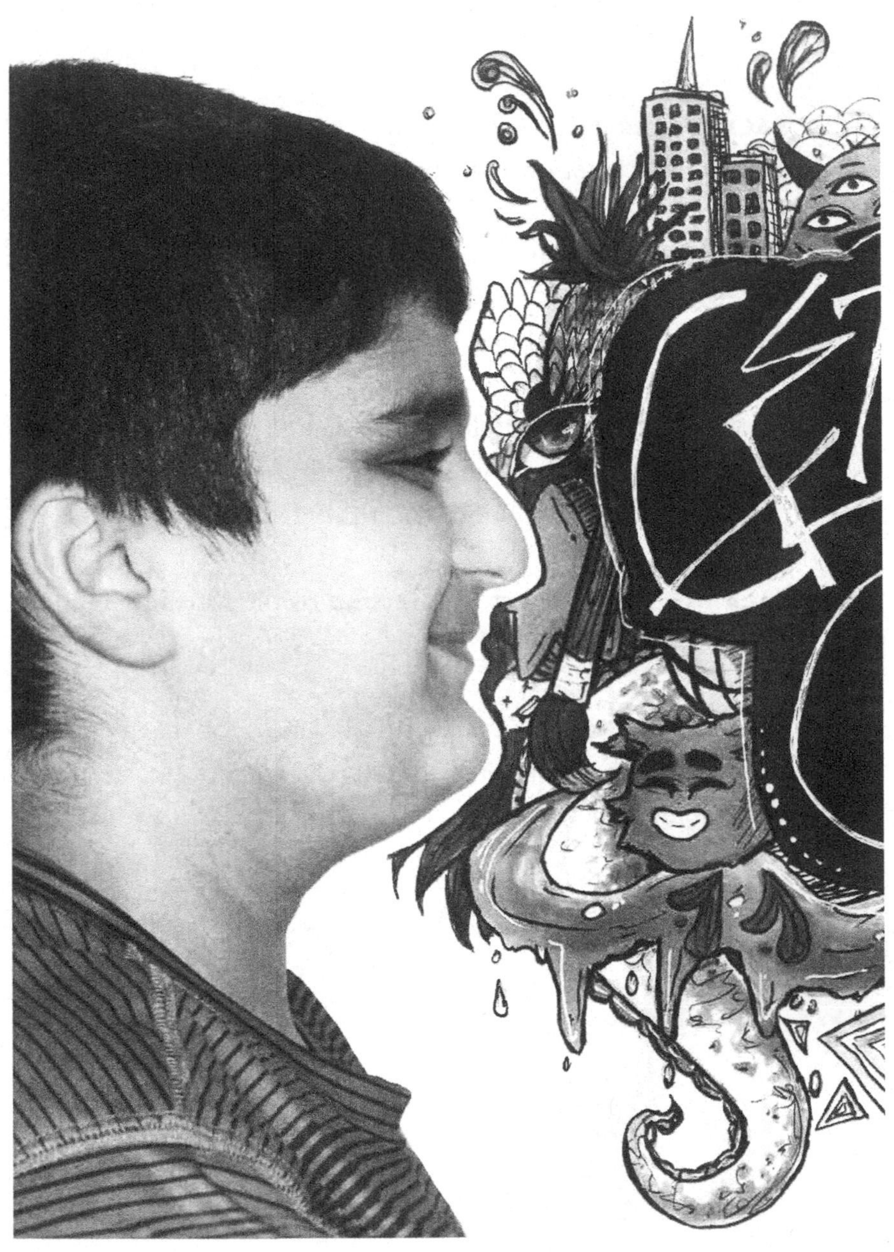

~~POINTLESS MESSAGES I SENT TO AN ADDRESS IN HEAVEN~~

~~Things i would love for people to know~~

~~REMEMBER ME THIS WAY WHEN I DIE~~

TITLE TEXT HERE

Salihah Aakil

In my house singing is like breathing. It is something that is always done, that has always been done, and that we will never stop doing. Essential and adored. Several times a day my siblings and I break into song, loud, clear, and somewhat off-key. Dancing to the vibrations from our bluetooth speaker. An outsider would think we planned these things, but we never do. Music is just something that has always been a part of us, so much so that we often fall asleep and wake up to music, our hearts doing their best to mimic drums. Music is our worship, our freedom, our hope, and love. This fact is one of great importance because to know me, dear reader, you must first know the extent of the joy I feel while singing. The extent of the love I feel for my family, the way being with them makes me feel like I have wings, and how desperately

I have always wanted to fly. I have prayed to God for wings many a time, not only as a child. Just this year I asked for wings hoping that if I didn't get them here, then maybe if I got to heaven Allah would gift them to me there. But a speaker sits in my living room for whenever I'm feeling caged. And for now I have a voice, two hands, and a home, and I will call that freedom until I learn otherwise.

These wings are invisible to the ungrateful eye.

Months ago my sisters and I attempted to take a photo. One that featured a girl blowing glitter —maybe stardust— from her hands into a camera. I was the model, my older sister the photographer, my younger one her assistant. We collected glitter from the bottoms of old craft drawers, unearthing memory and dust from the depths of our childhood. We gathered cloth to prevent the glitter from covering everything and we set to work. It was work. Much more than we would have thought. I blew the glitter into the camera, my sisters held up a blinding light and worried about the camera lens in turn. I made faces when I shouldn't, we yelled and laughed, it took way too long. And despite all of our best efforts, despite all the precautions we took, glitter got everywhere. In part because of my fumble-fingered fail, but mostly because that's just what glitter does. We ended with a photo none of us had expected and a decision to walk to the park in below-freezing weather, because we'd do anything for art. We still sparkled from amusement and glitter. And the walls still sparkled, and the couch still sparkled, and the glitter would remain there for days to come as a reminder of how hard we tried to shine.

We're still trying.

For as long as I can remember my nickname has always been Sasa. I don't know why. When I ask, my mom says her best friend gave the name to me, she says I was barely two months old when it happened. Most kids grow to hate their childhood nicknames, but I can confidently say that I love mine, it's as much a part of me as any of my names. I consider it my shield, the name I give to protect S A L I H A H from the constant butchering it receives from the tongues of the ignorant, uncaring, or innocent. The ones who find the syllables too foreign. You know, the ones who can't quite fathom how a girl like me can walk around with a name so mahogany and gold. Salihah Amaal Aakil. A monument to my mother, my people, and myself.

I would tell you if you asked.

You know, it must be weird not to fear the cops. Strange not to jump at the sounds of sirens or wonder which one of your people they have come to take away. I think about these things some nights, like there is someone somewhere who takes comfort in one of my greatest fears. I guess that just goes to show how utterly inescapable existing as one's self is, how trapped we are as ourselves. You as you. Me as me. How for me to learn your existence is impossible. And for you to understand the full extent of mine cannot be done. Human beings existing singularly as what we are, caged. And that cop will never know the basis of my fear, not to the full extent. And I will never know the basis of the cop's... fear, hate, misunderstanding? And so I'm left with the paradox of an outsider, too outside to understand, yet unable to get close. And I will never understand you as you, 'you' is something inherently out of reach. I can never truly walk in your shoes.

And yet I've spent my whole life trying.

As a kid, I always imagined God as a blue apparition. He never had a face with features, but was so tall and so wide that he spanned all of creation. This "God" didn't have feet either, he had a body that ended in a sort of wisp the way the ancestors from Mulan did. I guess it's borderline blasphemous to compare Allah to a cartoon, but my childhood mind couldn't comprehend him any other way. Back then I pictured God in a *kufi*, and when they told me he was everywhere I imagined him covering the whole globe with his mist-like body. Thought maybe he was always giving me a hug. When they said he loved hearing the prayers of children I decided that I was set for at least a few more years. Like "He already loves me? Great, I ain't even done nothing yet." As a kid I had my own prayer rug, small and impractical, but I loved it with all my heart. Red like life, fringed like all of the fanciest things, and I prayed to Allah in the best way I knew how. With the best understanding I could have of him, the blue, misty man who wasn't a man, and protected me in his constant embrace.

Sometimes I regret growing up.

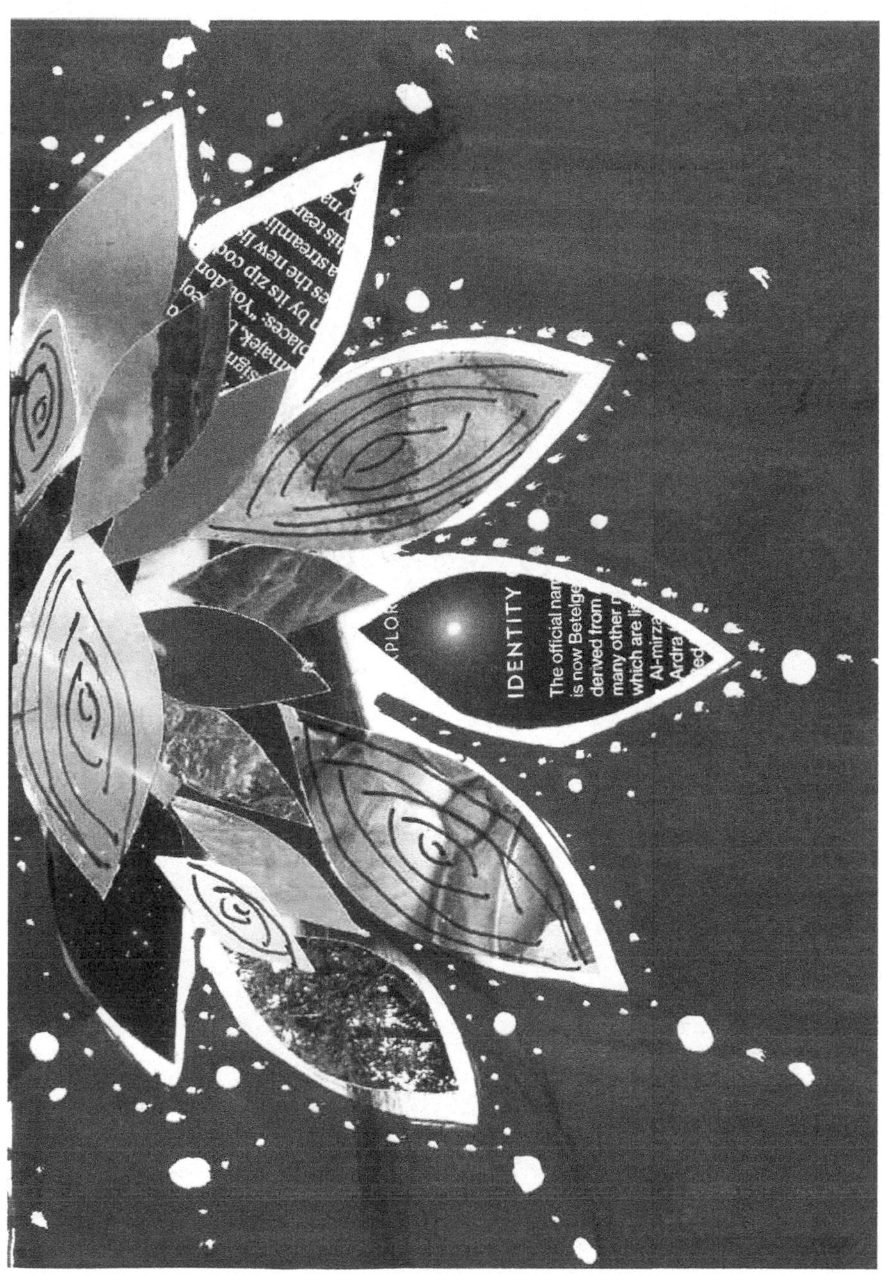
IDENTITY

Prayer Rug

Noor Saleem

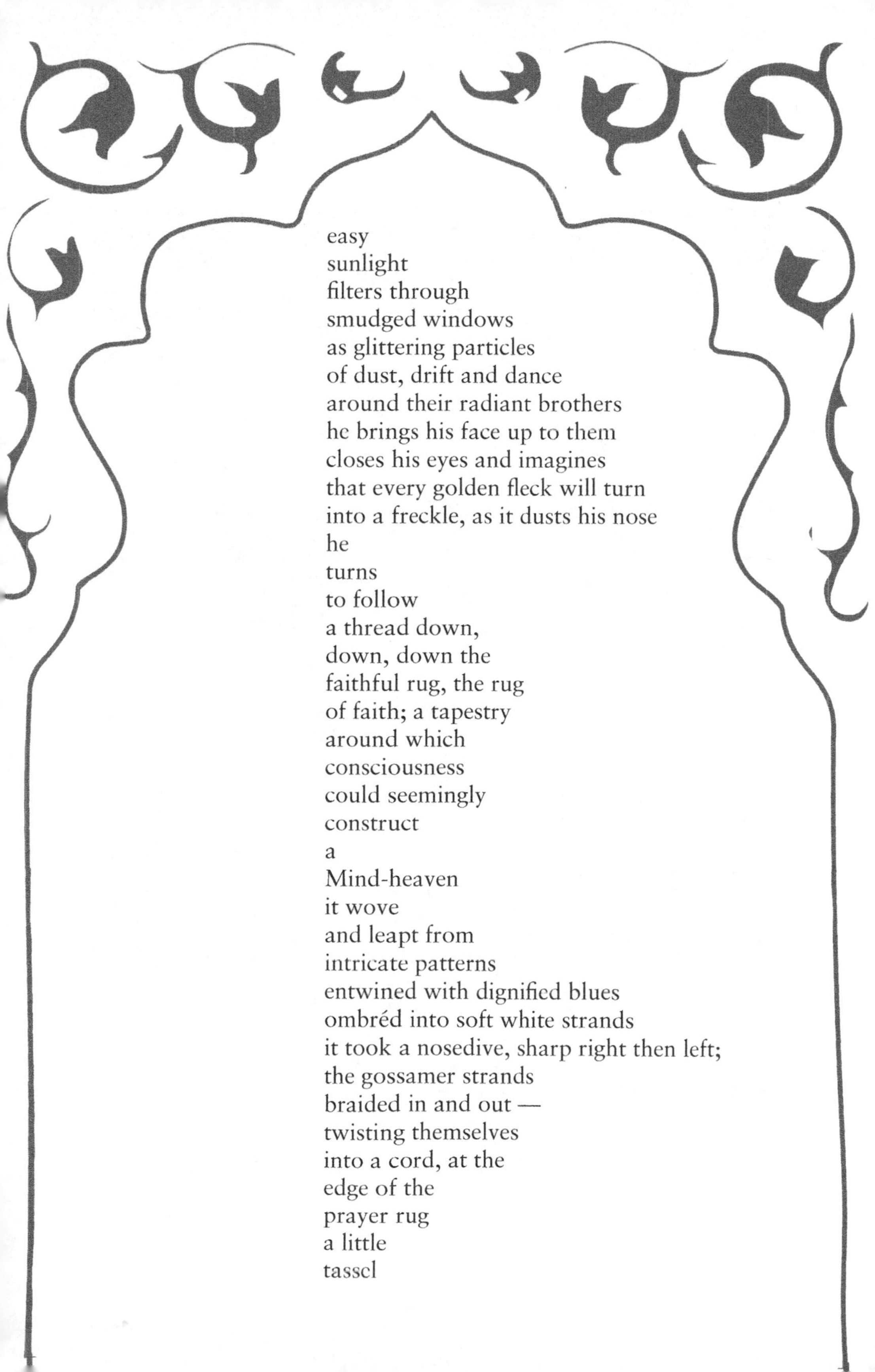

easy
sunlight
filters through
smudged windows
as glittering particles
of dust, drift and dance
around their radiant brothers
he brings his face up to them
closes his eyes and imagines
that every golden fleck will turn
into a freckle, as it dusts his nose
he
turns
to follow
a thread down,
down, down the
faithful rug, the rug
of faith; a tapestry
around which
consciousness
could seemingly
construct
a
Mind-heaven
it wove
and leapt from
intricate patterns
entwined with dignified blues
ombréd into soft white strands
it took a nosedive, sharp right then left;
the gossamer strands
braided in and out —
twisting themselves
into a cord, at the
edge of the
prayer rug
a little
tassel

In the name of God, the Beneficent, the Merciful

Salihah Aakil

Fajr
the white thread of dawn

Cold water
cold air on cold cheeks reminds us
"prayer is better than sleep"
darkness and sweet dreams stepping into the light
eyelids heavy dreams forgotten to soon be prayer-worthy
golden light a promise
prayer rugs mimic blankets
blankets forget our shape
warmth retreats
prayer is better than sleep
Fatiha reminds us of all we've been given
here and alive rubbing sleep from our eyes
here to watch the morning come.

Dhuhr
the bright light of noon

Family, together, standing on prayer rugs
that rival the finest creations.
Heads on *torbah*,
Eyes seeing beyond what is known to us.
Holding hands, smiling eyes,
singing in the spaces between ayat.
Tell me this is not perfect union.
Tell me this is not what we remember
from the days before hatred.
Home is where this is,
this resides in our homes. Tall and forever.
A drumbeat to knock our hearts off tempo.

Asr
the red disk of evening

Sun sings to accompany this recitation.
This gemstone language from a holy source.
Sun smiles to warm my back.
Responds to my *Allahuakbar* with a wry "Than what?"
Sun rays spread dust moats through my living room.
I frown like they haven't always been there.
Sun glints off of the shine of my dhikr beads and I tell her
Red has always been the color of worship.
I tell her *La ilaha illallah*, and Sun says,
"Yes, and there is no God who doesn't love you."

Maghrib
the relief of iftar

Warm hands on warm rugs remind us of all this blessing.
Greeting *Layl* with a confirmation that everything is complete.
Padded floors on tired knees, an ending.
A glorious reward for what we used to do.
A letting go of sunshine, and basking in a golden goodbye.
And we join in this and afterward,
never to let go the memory of being together.
Never to let go what has brought us together.
And we laugh and eat and *Alhamdulillah*
can be heard throughout the night.

Isha
the deep blue of night

Prayer rugs mimicking blankets, *Ash hadu anla ilaha illallah.*
Protected.
Here we sleep.
Blue is the memory of what was owed,
what will be owed again.
Layl beckons to us.
Beckons the blankets that forgot our place in them.
Our place is here.
Prayer is better than sleep,
Sleep is mercy.
In the name of Allah the Beneficent, the Merciful.

If I told you
would you
heart to
America

I AM A MAN
I AM A MUSLIM

Hands up...
in prayer
in Sajdah
don't shoot

I AM...

i am
i am
i am

i am
i am
i am

حسين
حسين
حسين
حسين
that I love you...
find it in your
let me breathe,
?

Imaan Shanavas

Underground was a beautiful place. Not in the way that Aboveground was. There wasn't a blue sky, or green grass, or fluffy white clouds that took on different shapes according to each child's imagination. But there was sunlight, rays of sunlight that shot through the holes above. The children loved to stand in the sunlight. They would let the warmth engulf their faces and the light blind them so that they could see nothing, feel nothing, but a gold haze washing over. At night, the rays of daylight would leave, but they were replaced by moonbeams, incandescent, where even the adults couldn't help but dance.

Twice a year, the community would come together in celebration of *Loloor*, a festival of lights and colors. Vibrant banners ran from store to store. Children barreled through the streets, painted in rainbows from head to toe, proudly waving glowing Undergrounder flags. Neighbors teamed up to cook for everyone: sweet salwa, spicy mesla, and bowls of steaming sayba. At night everyone Underground assembled to sing and dance under colored lanterns strung overhead. Underground was beautiful in the way that it sheltered a group of people, beautiful in the way it kept them safe, and provided them with food, connection, community.

Until now.

The oxygen levels were plummeting. Children who used to bask in the glow of the sun now resided in makeshift infirmaries. Their small bodies that used to dance under moonbeams now lay in hospital beds, lifeless. Their formerly rosy skin had now become a flushed blue. Their voices that used to laugh and shriek now wept for their parents, who were suffering in rooms nearby. Victims of hypoxia now aimlessly roamed the streets amidst the rubble.

Neighbors who were once like family were now competitors. A shortage of oxygen masks led to fights between parents, all of whom were desperate to secure lifelines for their children. But even these escapes were temporary: the masks would run out of oxygen, too. Citizens became more and more desperate as they found themselves burying more and more of their loved ones. The government lost control as the bodies began to pile up. The oxygen crisis spared no one. Not children, not the elders, not the rich. Underground was no longer survivable.

They would have to come up.

Radios Aboveground casually reported the harrowing situation below. Some nations declared they would receive the Undergrounders with open arms. Others were not so accepting. The Chancellor of the Combined Provinces of Liberty blasted warnings from the speakers: "I will not compromise the safety of my citizens for some red-eyed devils."

The "red-eyed devils" were the majority of the Underground population. Their rare eye color set them apart, making them OTHER, and therefore feared. At dinner tables Aboveground, some families discussed the oxygen crisis out of obligation, or guilt, but would quickly turn to lighter subjects. News anchors demonstrated compassion through tears and spurious laments—"It's just horrible!"—before moving on to discuss the weather. Citizens would read about the agony of the poor children beneath them, shake their head in solidarity, then toss the newspaper aside and proceed with their day. Others weren't even willing to do that. Some thought that the oxygen crisis was merely a conspiracy, that the Undergrounders had ulterior motives for coming up. They were said to be radical, haters of Abovegrounders and everything the CPL stood for. They were *dangerous*. So how could individual people be expected to be sympathetic? Most of them had probably never even met an Undergrounder. And never would.

But you did.

* * *

You could see two, no three, figures cowering behind the trees.

"Who's there?" you called.

Shakily, the children emerged from behind the stumps. The oldest one could not have been much older than you. Her soft face was etched with suffering. Two smaller children trembled behind her, peeking out from behind her skirt. They were Undergrounders. You knew it. You knew it and you couldn't turn away.

Despite their squinting from the blazing sun, you could still see their eyes. Bright pink. Not red. Pink. A beautiful pink, a pink of innocence. You couldn't help but get closer. The Undergrounders stood frozen; they did not retreat.

Their eyes were stunning: the color of roses, coral, hydrangea. You were reminded of summer sunsets and the azaleas your grandmother grew in the springtime. Nothing to fear. And despite the magnificence of these eyes, you could now also see their anguish. The soft sun that used to provide the Undergrounders with warmth and joy had now become ruthless, burning their delicate pale skin red. Their thin legs seemed ready to give way. You couldn't imagine the pain they were in, and didn't want to.

The little girl began fiddling nervously with something around her neck. It was a silver locket with a blue stone in the center that almost seemed to glow against her skin. Your hand instantly jumped to your own locket, which had been hanging from your neck since the day your mother gave it to you. It was almost identical to hers except for the center stone. Whose picture did she hold in hers? Was it her father? Who gave her the locket? Her mother? Where were they? Your thoughts were interrupted by the girl's delicate voice.

"Are you going to hurt us?" she asked.

"Shhhh," said the oldest.

They stared at you, trembling, and you stared at them, trembling, too.

What to do? Contact the authorities? That would most definitely hurt them. But wasn't that what you'd been advised to do? Everything you'd seen in the media ping-ponged in your head: newspapers, television, radio. Red-eyed people. Desperate. Dangerous. Untrustworthy. It struck you that you'd never seen a photograph, no close-up of their faces. Any renderings of the Undergrounders were illustrations. Drawings, paintings, sculptures, but never photographs. Why?

In school, too, you'd learned to fear the Undergrounders. Your teachers didn't dare express their explicit aversion, but their tone was often bitter, detached, dismissive. Was it possible that they had been wrong? No. That would mean the whole school system was wrong and that couldn't be right. There had to be some other explanation.

Maybe these three were the exception to the red eye standard. That had to be it. After all there had to be a reason why the Chancellor was so opposed to them... Right?

You looked the Undergrounders in the eye. Their fate was in your hands. You had the power here. You had the power and it was terrifying.

You took one last look at their stricken faces and glittering eyes.

Then you slowly turned and walked away.

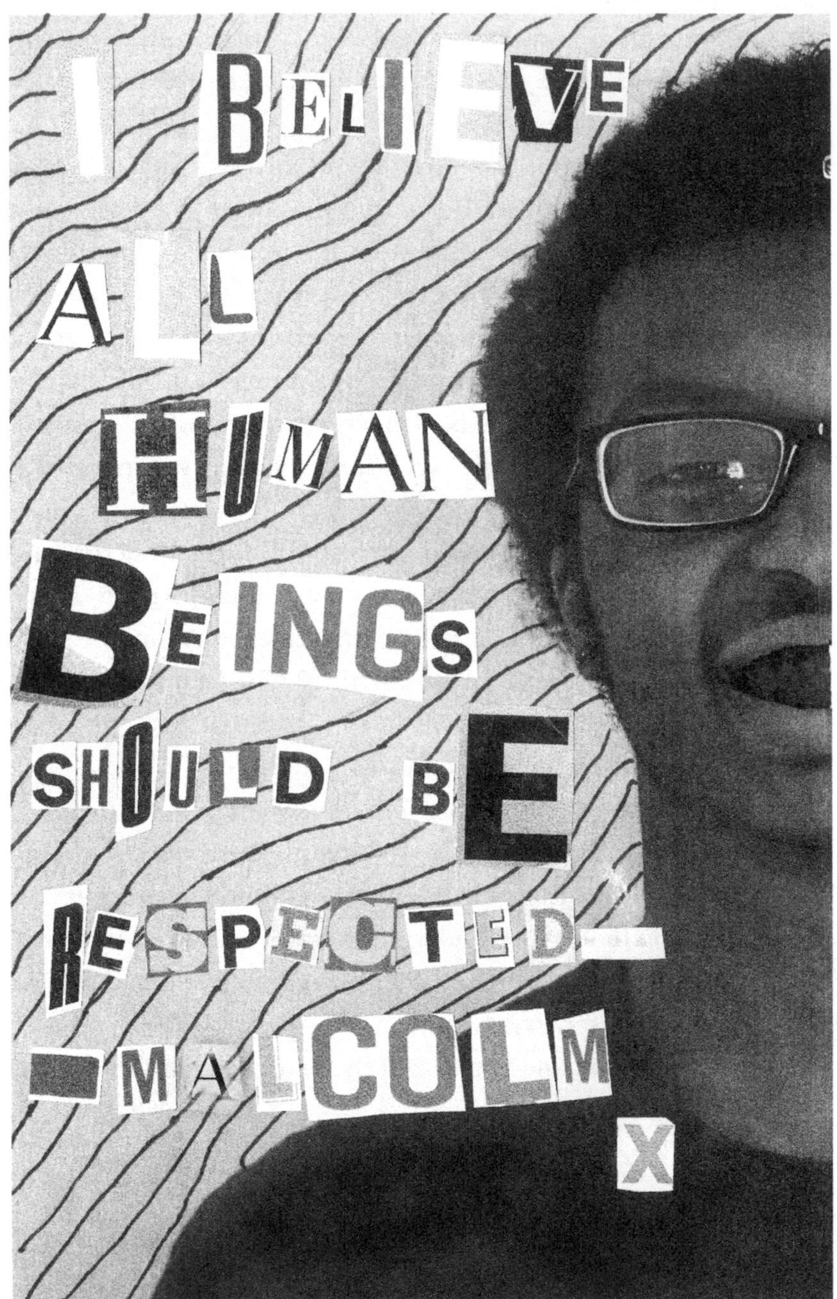
I BELIEVE
ALL
HUMAN
BEINGS
SHOULD BE
RESPECTED
—MALCOLM
X

YOU CAN'T TOUCH MY HAIR
I AM WHO I AM

Name: Salihah A.

Worksheet No. 2

Fill in the Blanks:

They can never get my ________ right.

Name Race Age Story

They don't believe me when I tell them I am __________ It hurts.

Muslim Proud Open-minded Unchained Sorry Not sorry Awake

Vocabulary:

1. Define Yourself.

2. Define America.

3. Define Peace and use it in a sentence.

4. Define what Islam means to you and use it in a sentence.

Multiple Choice:

1. To be Muslim and to be American is to…
    a. Be treated as foreign even at home
    b. Be free
    c. Be caged
    d. Be the rope in a game of tug-of-war
    e. Be misunderstood
    f. Be at peace
    g. Be

2. Most days I am murdered by…
    a. Hate
    b. Ignorance
    c. Misinformation
    d. Malice
    e. Misunderstanding

3. They assumed me…
    a. Stupid
    b. Homophobic
    c. Hateful
    d. Terrorist
    e. Intelligent
    f. Hopeful
    g. Kind
    h. None of these
    i. Something different

4. Me + Islam =
   a. Identity
   b. Peace
   c. Justice
   d. Home
   e. Conflict
   f. Stability
   g. Something different

Essay Questions:

What does all of this mean to you?

Who do you love, who loves you?

Who told you what the right path was, why did you choose this one?

Do you believe this is right?

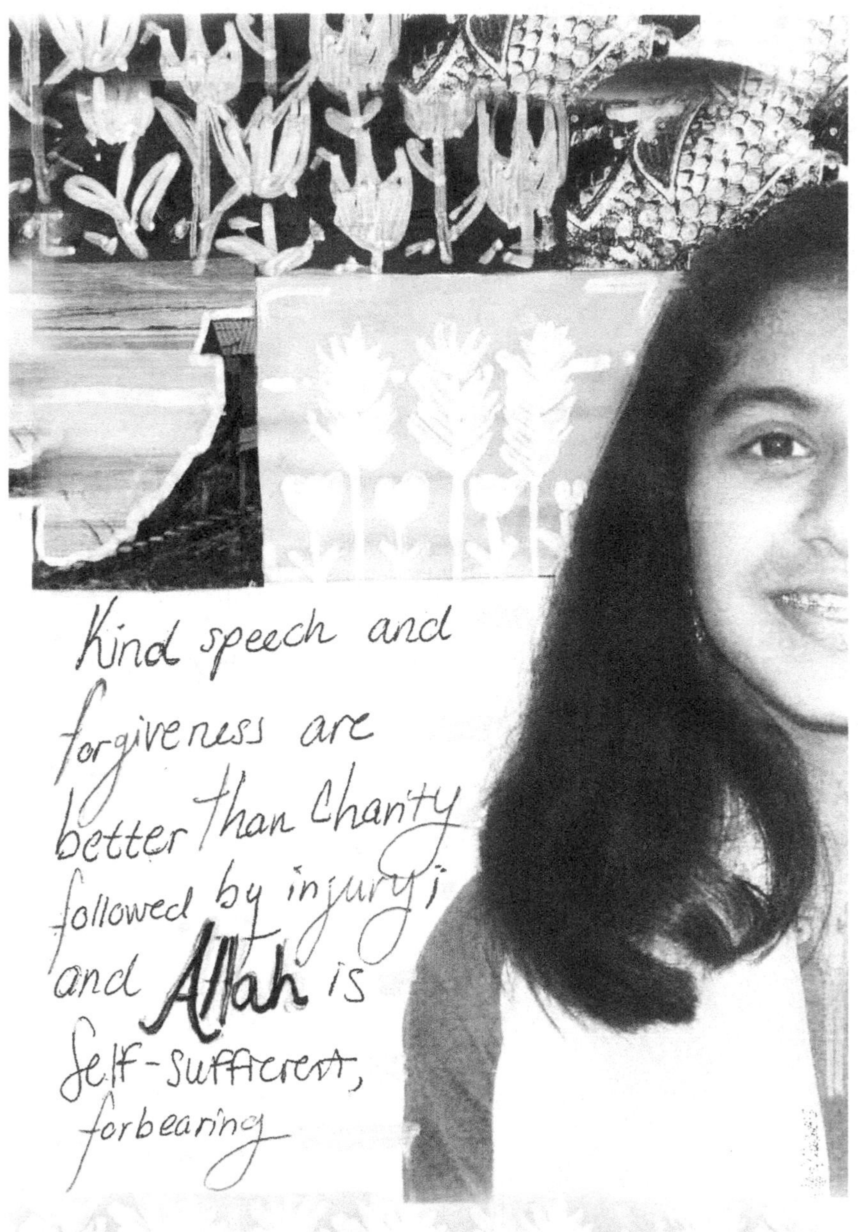
Kind speech and
forgiveness are
better than Charity
followed by injury;
and Allah is
Self-sufficient,
forbearing

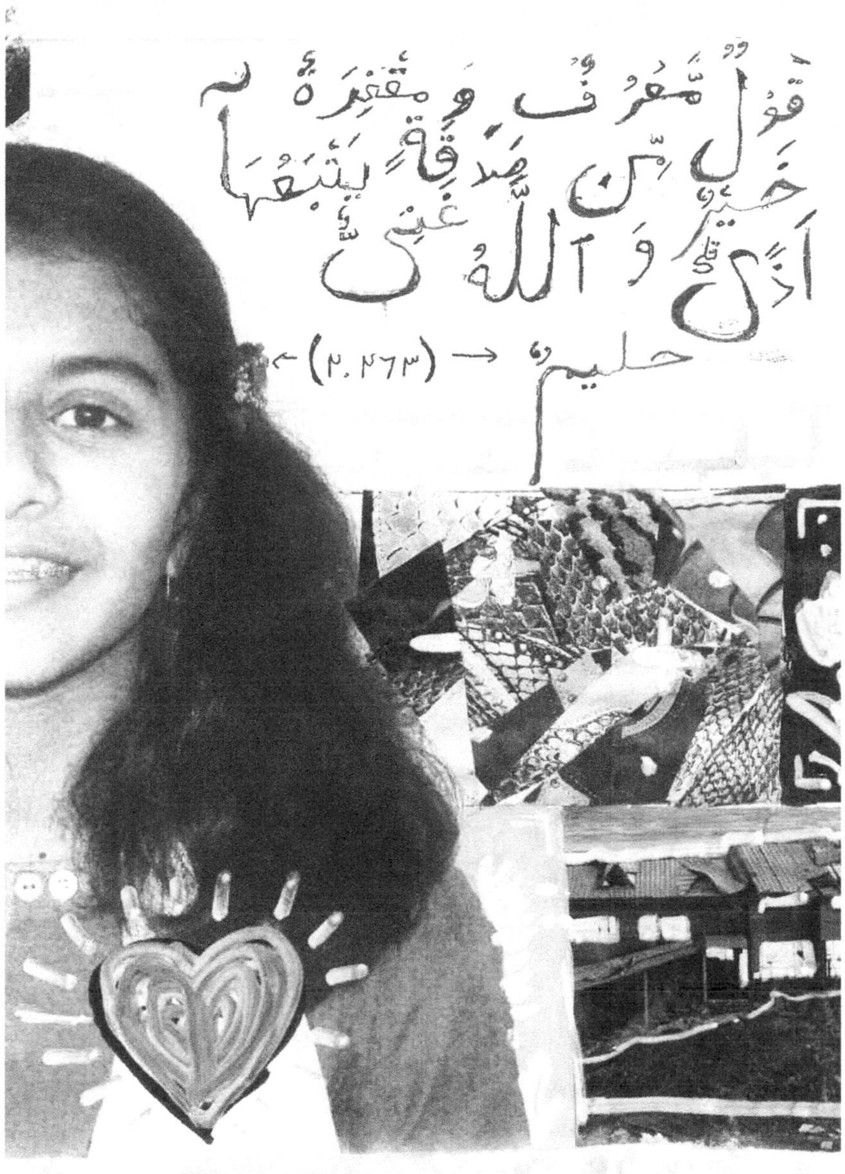
قول معروف ومغفرة
خير من صدقة يتبعها
أذى والله غني
حليم (٢.٢٦٣)

hy·phen
/ˈhīfən/
noun
1. the sign -, used to join words to indicate their combined meaning or that they are linked in the grammar of a sentence
2. to indicate the division of a word at the end of a line
3. to indicate a missing or implied element

by Noor Saleem

what missing element of my identity are you trying to
compensate for?

soft-spoken
pitch-black
razor-sharp
cold-hearted
skin-deep
self-conscious
narrow-minded
muslim-american

muslim
+
american

a couplet of confused words
connected by
a little hyphen
who in marrying them
who in its conjoining, leashing, connecting
has overpowered
and powered-over
who I am
who am I?

I wonder,
little hyphen
do you bring my two worlds together,
or separate them?

I just want you
to know, hyphen,
that your hovering presence
is very much
not appreciated.

RUQAYYAH AAKIL

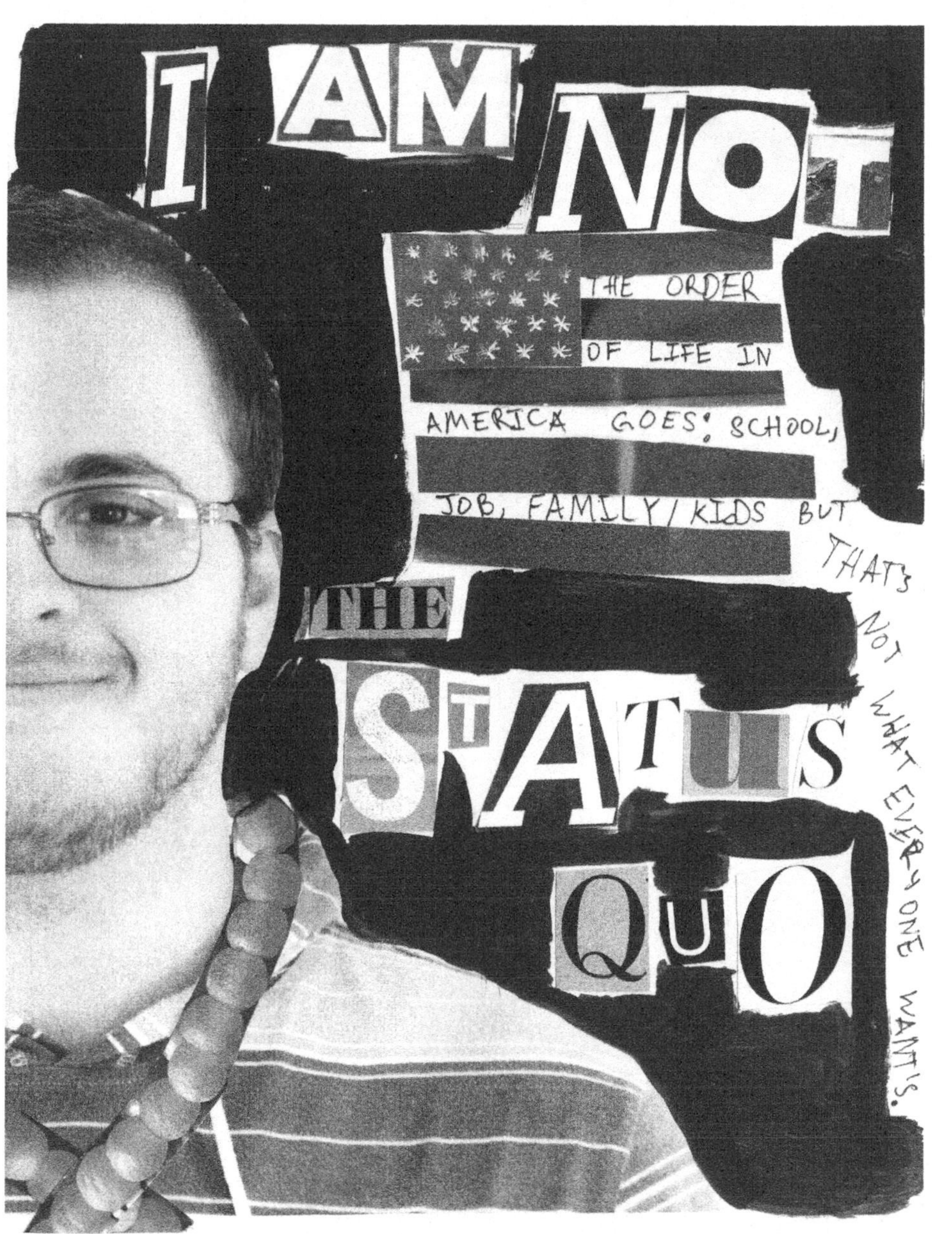

Moments I Remember I'm Muslim

Leyla Rasheed

When It's Hot

On the hottest days, I think to myself
What are shorts for?
I mean for my Muslim American teenage girl self,
the self where I make my **own** decisions
to fit my **own** identity.

Most days, I don't wear them.
(I want to follow my religious responsibilities.)
But some days, I must.
I play sports, so some days I'm an athlete first,
Muslim second.

I know it doesn't sound like much,
or even a topic worth discussing.
But certain times I feel eyes looking at me,
like on those hot days when I'm wearing jeans,
like ***Why aren't you wearing shorts?***

On those days I get comments like,
Aren't you hot in that?
or
How are you wearing pants?

I mean how do I respond?
oh, I feel more spiritually connected when
more covered?
Like, how can I say that?

Instead I say:
I didn't know it was going to be hot,
or
My legs don't get hot.
Even though that's not true.

I mean I don't want to just sit there and explain
how I choose not to wear shorts,
because then I have to get into
why I don't wear shorts for school,
but why I do for gym,
and why for other sports,
that's a different story,
and then finally I'm explaining my entire
culture and **religion**.
NO.

It's not that I'm embarrassed of being a Muslim American,
of grandparents from India and Pakistan,
but that I have to explain something
that anyone else wouldn't even
THINK of having to clarify.

Don't get me wrong.
I like being unique and having my differences,
but sometimes it's the little things,
like having to explain a personal matter to the world,
that get to me.

Now it's my turn to ask:
Why is my religion questioned
by people who go day-to-day
without having to explain a single part
of their lifestyle?

Why am I singled out for **everyone** to watch?

When It's Homecoming

My friends get their dresses from Lulus,
        a popular online boutique.

The only problem is that EVERYONE,
        and I mean everyone,
        gets their dress from there.
So if you want to twin with someone,
        Lulus is the place to go.

But for me,
        I go with whatever my mom finds
        that I can agree with.

The undefined rule in our house,
        that I've kind of gotten used to
        and I don't really mind,
        is jumpsuits and maxi dresses
        are the move.

I wish it wasn't the case,
        I mean it's hard enough
        being a little freshman in high school
        but I just flow with it.
This isn't too much of a problem for me
        because I like the jumpsuits I find.

My friends think I'm very fashion-forward.

I know people must wonder,
Why does she never show her legs?
But when they talk to me it's usually just things like,
Ugh, why do you look so good in jumpsuits?

I know they are trying to be nice,
but it feels almost like a shallow comment,
or like they are trying to point out that
I LOOK DIFFERENT
from everyone else.

I mean obviously,
sometimes,
I wish I could just pull off
a nice Lulus dress,
one that would make me feel like
I'm in.

But then I realize that
in whatever outfit I choose,
I can feel confident,
and I enjoy that feeling
OF BEING DIFFERENT
with my own style.

When I'm Fasting

I have been lucky enough
to be able to fast during school,
which I know doesn't sound too great,
but trust me
being busy for more than half the day
is better than being stuck at home
with a fridge full of food

that
I.
can't.
eat.

I actually even like lunchtime
when I'm fasting
because I get to hang out with my friends
and I don't even look at the clock
e v e r y   t h r e e   s e c o n d s
to see if time has passed.

Obviously,
when I show up to lunch one day
without my fake Vera Bradley lunch bag
I get **LOTS** of questions.

I try to alert my friends a few days before

If I don't explain how fasting works
my socializing hour will be taken up
with talk like

Not even water!
Isn't that a health hazard?
Doesn't your stomach hurt?

It is quite hard to answer some comments,
not that they're mean or rude
but just because
there really is no way to answer

and it makes you wonder,

What do people think about me?
Do they think that my parents are forcing me?
Or do they understand
that I make my own decisions,
and I know what is best?

I want to respond to all these questions,
but while I'm fasting,
one might notice that
I talk much less,
and I'm doing this
for the benefit of the other person.

(No one wants a whiff
of Faster's Breath
from close proximity.)

My friends also say stuff like

I should do this with you,
Might shed a few pounds.

Hmmm.

Personally,
I like it when we can lighten the mood
but sometimes I can't help but think,
Am I a joke to them?
Is my religion a joke to them?
Is the way I live my life everyday...
a joke to them?

And fasting is not just physical,
you know,
it's not just not eating.

It's also about staying away from anything bad
like lying
and gossip
and meanness.

The mental aspects of fasting are the hardest.

As much as it seems like staying away from gossip is easy,
not knowing the tea
of the inner circle?
Now, that's a challenge
for my teenage girl self.

It's true that fasting can be hard,
but at the end of the day
I choose to go with it
because it's **fulfilling.**

I take pride
in being able to accomplish
something
that reminds me
who I am.

When It's Eid

Getting up at 6 a.m. is tough,
but I love it,
waking up early,
straightening my hair,
adding some touches of makeup
here and there,
and very carefully—
as they are prone to ripping—
putting on my Pakistani outfit.

I look forward to checking my henna in the morning.

When we go to the mosque,
it is a sea of people,
all in their unique color outfits.

If you are seeing an Eid gathering for the first time,
you might think we look like a human rainbow.

And you will also undoubtedly think,
There is absolutely no space in here.
(It can get suffocating.)

But it's also nice, too,
knowing that there are so many people,
whom I have never met,
who have the same religious beliefs
and such a strong connection with God,
that we are willing to sweat together
for prayer.

The party officially starts around 10:00,
but since Desis are always running late,
no one really arrives until
10:45 or even...
11:00.
(If people really did show up on time,
nothing would be set up
because running late and not being ready
is also part of our crazy family.
Welcome!)

It can be awkward, at first,
like when your mom introduces you
to someone you have
never
seen in your life,
and you are pulled
into a
hard and long
embrace
for what seems like hours.

But then, when my all my friends arrive,
Muslim and non-Muslim,
First-timers and every-timers,
Mosque friends and school friends,
I bounce from one group to another,
taking pictures, playing games.

Will they like the food? I wonder,
but no need to worry,
as they fill their plates
with steaming hot piles of rice, chicken, aloo, poori.

Wow! This food is really good!
They say, and
I smile.

I am the only brown person in my friend group,
and it feels nice to show them
that there are many of us,
that the Muslim community
is so much bigger
than just me.

At Eid I remember what I love
about being Muslim, like
that we welcome everyone,
that we are a community,
and that we all celebrate
Together.

HOW
DO I
BALA
MY
W
"What are
Shorts for?...
I mean for My
Muslim American
teenage Self."

NCE
ORLDS?

Noor Saleem

I never used to talk
about my identity,
my ethnicity,
my religion.
I didn't talk about
where I came from
and who I was,
so I grew to forget
those parts of me.
I diminished their value;
I discredited them
until their meaning
began to deteriorate.
I left them
to the back of my mind,
because
if they weren't important
enough to be asked about,
then they weren't important
enough for me to remember.

No one asked,
and by the agency
of that acute silence
I began to feel
a kind of desolation
that only comes from
being solitary.
A desolation that comes with
the singularity of moving
through a crowd;
the steady, onward
flow of the masses
did not change my feeling
of misdirection.

I could feel the loneliness
in my bones, that ached
with the exhaustion
of being forcibly detached
from their mother,
my home,
where I came from,
the timeworn beauty
of my story.

They didn't ask,
but I had to tell them;
I had to tell them
what I was, who I was,
as an act of remembrance.
Because,
without this declaration,
my own self
could not accept itself;
I didn't know
my own name;
and I found myself speaking
in unnatural tongue
when I longed to
breathe flowers.

The mourning
of my lost identity
yielded numbness,
so that
all I was made of
was a faint echo
of my story.

And, I didn't even know
if I would be whole
If I told them
that it would complete me
the same way, in the same
capacity as if it had never
been lost
To the same extent that it had
been taken from me
Taken of me

After its swells overcame me;
I knew that truth of self
never came peacefully.

I had to command myself,
I had to remind myself
to coax out the memory
of who I was;
I had to sing my name
to the stars,
and declare myself
to the stillness of the
night sky.

WHO
AM
I?
AM I?

Who

prayer

Salihah Aakil

When I was barely three years old my mother taught me how to pray.

Not as a ritual, not bowing and kneeling and standing back up, but the way only a three-year-old could. Soft hands, shining eyes, a heart too pure to sully the surface of her prayer rug.

My mother taught me how to pray for the people who might not rise with the sun in the morning, taught me how to pray for myself. I prayed before I slept, and whether I had good dreams or nightmares, I spent the night swaddled in hope and love.

She taught me how to make my wishes into beacons that would shine through the night.

How to heal bits of this devastated world with pleading eyes at daybreak. She said, "God loves answering the prayers of children."

My mother is a prayer. Part good intention and always knowing what's best. Part everlasting legacy and part miracle.

My mother is everlasting, through hard times that would have knocked most down but only made her want to keep going.

Through broken windows and broken glasses.

She prayed and stood with her back up straight and all of these years later I am learning to do the same.

unique
Living
Anchor
harmony
killed
captured 380
sheltered
Daily News.

Pride & Sticky Notes

Ayah Noor

What made me angry?

That was the question that kept floating through my mind as I went home from Friday's youth group. It was the question sister Maha, our group leader, had asked us to ask ourselves for this week's project. Usually the project routine was the same: we read a page of the Qur'an, discussed a verse, and then sister Maha gave us a related assignment due the following week, like planting flowers or writing poems. But this week? She asked us to think about anger.

"What I *don't* want," sister Maha said, "is a rant about how your lives are unfair. I know you are teenagers, and this can be a time of great angst..." I half-laughed. This reminded me why our group was sometimes referred to as the sassy young lady group.

"Instead, I want you to speak for the truth and against the hate, even if your voice will shake."

Oh boy. There is *clearly* no pressure around here! But at least she rhymed.

***

The whole way home, I dramatically watched rain slide down the car windows. I thought about the project but had no idea what to do. I wanted to complain about all the things that annoyed me—like the sound of people chewing, or wide-ruled notebooks—but apparently those things weren't deep enough. I needed a purpose, something that boiled my blood. But what?

After a few hours at home procrastinating, I figured the only thing I could really do was ask God for help about my project... and then ask my mom, because she seemed to hold all the secrets of the universe.

I headed downstairs and was enveloped by the smell of mantu. "*Salaam Madar Jan!*" I said as I entered the kitchen. Mom was busy finishing up the beef filling. "Can you help me with something?" I asked.

"I'm kind of busy right now, what is it?"

"Well... sister Maha said our projects have to be about something that makes you angry, but I want it to be powerful and stuff, so do you have any ideas?"

She was occupied with another pot. "Hold on." She stirred it and took out the dough for the mantu. "Maybe you could try searching for some ideas on that tablet of yours? But try to do something that isn't too *dramatic*."

"When did I ever do something *dramatic*?" I asked. "I'll do a search, but I mean I won't be looking for things that are *happy*..."

"Asal, the meat will burn, what should I pay attention to? Just go search something and insha'Allah you'll eventually find something good. But when you're done, come down to fill these up with me."

I hugged her for the tip and went back upstairs to my room. I opened up Google and stared at the screen. What exactly was I searching for? I typed in: 'list of stuff that makes people angry.' Some options:

1. People leaving shopping carts in the middle of a parking lot
2. Being blamed for something you didn't do
3. Politicians
4. People who are talking during a movie

None of these were what I was looking for, but I still wrote them down anyway in my *college*-ruled notebook. Progress.

I scrolled down further and saw something else on that list.

Terrorists.

When I read that I felt a jolt in my gut. It didn't say terrorism. It said terrorists. I knew what was coming next. Right below that it said, "See also: Islamic terrorists."

I ignored this, just like I ignored hundreds of comments about terrorism and extremists that assumed these things were somehow connected to my faith. Why blame violence only on Islam? What about "See also: white supremacist terrorists"?

Anyway, there was no point sitting there worrying over everything, but the thought of what I read lingered.

I went on YouTube to try to clear my head. Which meant that first, like any responsible girl, I watched a video of how to contour your face to look like a pug. And then a compilation of babies falling on their faces. And then people planning a wedding, and then Japanese travel videos. And THEN I saw something that might actually be useful for the project: a video called the "Secret Life of Muslims."

I was struck by curiosity, mostly because I didn't think my life was all that interesting or secret. Maybe as a kid I might've pretended I was a spy, but now the only thing I did secretly was steal cookies from the cookie jar my mom hid under the couch. (Why under the couch? I don't know.) So I clicked on it.

I watched the first video of the series, and it was actually pretty good: basically a bunch of different people joking about the weirdest questions they were asked about being Muslim (like do we worship a Moon God?) and clarifying that there are like 1.7 billion of us out there, so, you know, it's tough to answer for everybody.

But then out of habit, I scrolled down to the comment section. That was another bad life decision right there. The only thing I saw was hate.

The comments went beyond 'go back to your country!' They said we were here to take over. That we would force our laws on everyone and impose our culture. That we could not be trusted. And too many other hateful, racist things that I don't want to repeat.

Basically a whole lot of people out there were quoting things they didn't understand, misinterpreting things they didn't know much about, and saying that what I'd believed in since the day I was born was a lie and a cult.

Is this what the world was really like?

If I walked around outside, was this what was going on in people's heads?

Were the smiles I got actually fake?

How could I possibly trust in a world where this is what people believed?

Honestly, I'd had enough. I'd had enough of staying calm

and ignoring insults and hoping people would accept me. My blood was boiling, and my purpose was found. Here was something that truly made me angry, a time for me to "speak the truth against the hate" (and yes, my voice would shake.) I'd found my project.

And yet, what *exactly* could I do? I knew I had to do something about those comments, but what? I had no idea how I could possibly get from how I felt at that moment to something impactful. I prayed to God to help me. How could I change this negative into a positive?

After making dua, I stared at the wall above my desk. A while ago I had stuck a sticky note there that was supposed to help me feel better about myself during the times of "oh my God I'm such a failure." (OK, so maybe *sometimes* I can be dramatic.) The sticky note said, "Positivity can be found in the most unexpected places."

You know how they say 'God works in mysterious ways?' Well, they're right. Because somehow just by looking at that sticky note, I suddenly knew exactly what I wanted to do.

I went to meet up with my friend Malak who was 16 and by far the most interesting person I'd ever met. She believed in the 'evil eye,' which was the second reason she wore eyeliner, after her first reason, which was for her angsty emo self. So far it didn't seem like a phase. (It is never a phase.)

We were in her room and she had her laptop open and was following along with a hijab tutorial on YouTube, but Malak's scarf was looking far from 'elegant drapery.'

"Ugh," she said. "Useless." She clicked on another one

and @WithLoveLeena chirped, "Asalaam Alaykum ladies, today I want to show you three effortless chiffon hijab styles!" Before Malak started another mistake I decided to start my interview.

"What's something you think people misjudge about you?" I asked in a British accent because 1) British accents are cool, and 2) this was my professional project interview, how else did you expect me to do it?

"I love wearing black, it's such a happy color but—"

I cut her off, "Didn't Morticia Addams say that?"

"Yeah, anyway, these days if someone sees me wearing my hijab and all black they just stare and look scared. They probably think I want to blow something up! But you can't determine if someone is good or bad by just looking at them."

I awkwardly gave her a post-it note. "Do you want to write that down? And maybe some more?"

"Uh... OK." She grabbed the stack and uncapped her marker. "This is for your project, right? You know you still haven't told me what exactly it is you're doing."

"Right, because it's kind of stupid and I'm worried everyone will start laughing." I hid my face in her pillow.

"If it's like that how about I don't waste a perfectly good post-it note and you just don't do anything at all?"

"OK, OK. I wanted to, in a way, y'know... reverse all the hateful comments I read online." Malak nodded and smiled so I continued. "I figured I could create a wall of sticky-notes of *positive* things about Muslims, kind of like our own real life comment board."

"That's a great idea!" She grabbed a handful of sticky notes and wrote on each one. "Here," she said, "I hope it's enough."

I thanked her and felt myself swell up with what seemed to be a mixture of joy, pride, and excitement, so I suppose you could just say loads of good vibes.

I wondered if anyone would expect good vibes from someone dressed in all black.

Never in my life did I think I would be inside a gym. And I'm not talking about the super friendly spin class and treadmill gyms you see in the commercials during January, I'm talking about the ones with the heavy weights and the boxing bags and the creepy muscular guys. But I was there to see a friend of mine named Muska who boxed, and who was the definition of awesome. I'd told her about my project, and she immediately said she was in.

We sat in the corner of the boxing ring for our interview, and I couldn't help looking around and staring at all the intense people doing sit-ups and jumping rope and punching bags. "This place is awesome!" I said. "How do you stay modest while doing all these things?"

"I had to learn to layer things but there are times when it's hard. Like for example, I want to show off my six pack, buuuuut I can't." She smiled.

I awkwardly slid a post-it note over to her. "So, could you maybe write some things down, like we talked about?"

"Sure, on the phone you said you wanted positive messages about being Muslim, right?"

I nodded and watched as she wrote. She filled up one post-it, then another, then another. She handed them to me with a smile.

"Thanks!" I said. I read them over quickly. One said, "I love how forgiving the religion is. In Islam you learn how merciful God is, and how he understands we are all human." Another one said, "Being a Muslim keeps me grounded."

Ladies and gentlemen, this is what I call work in progress.

***

By Thursday, the stack of post-it notes I had started off with were now filled with positive comments, quotes, and doodles. I had asked almost every single person I knew in my community to help out with this, and over time the project grew into something I hadn't expected. I was excited, but there was also a lot of work to be done.

I had two stacks of sticky notes and a *giant* poster board. It took me a while to put everything together because I found myself reading each note and remembering how I got them. Every single post-it held a memory.

I held one that was written with messy handwriting, the one that my friend Hadya wrote while she was on the swings and I hung upside down from the monkey bars waiting for her to finish: "It feels like we're all one big squad, all there for each other."

Sara, who's the cutest 4-year-old ever, drew a whole bunch of scribbly hearts on one. One of my friends, Fatimah, wrote, "I fangirl just like you." That one made me laugh. It's like she was telling the world the supposed 'big secret' Muslim women hid under their scarves. We totally fangirl.

And sister Jamila wrote, "I think it's cool how we give a fellow Muslim we see in public a nod or smile even if we don't know them." I loved that, too, it gives such a sense of community.

The one my mother wrote reflected a soul that had gone through so much. She'd been a refugee from Afghanistan, and holds her homeland close to her heart. Her note was more like a message about how all of us can be better people: "I didn't come here out of choice, but you can choose the way you treat me."

Finally, there was just one remaining empty space on the poster. My space. I pulled out a sticky note, uncapped my marker, and wrote my little heart out.

I stared at the words I'd managed to cram onto the paper and Oh my Allah it was so cheesy it made me lactose intolerant. Yet I felt a sense of pride, too. I remembered a quote I'd seen once on Pinterest: "If you want to be irreplaceable, you must be different."

By the time I was done it was midnight. Somehow this project had turned from a typical youth group assignment into something I wanted the world to see. It felt so good to finish, like for so long I had been grasping for something that I couldn't reach, and finally, I got it.

Friday rolled around pretty fast and there I was, the only girl in the room holding a giant poster board when everyone else had a list scribbled on a page ripped out of a notebook. I wish there was someone else who did something like this!

Oh no, oh no, oh no, oh no, oh no, oh no, oh no, oh no, oh no, oh no, oh no, oh no, oh no, oh no, oh no, oh no, oh no.

Why did I do this? What was I thinking?

Sister Maha stood at the front and welcomed everyone.

"Asalaam Alaykum, girls and their lovely mothers!" She gave all the moms a kind smile and continued. "Today is a bit unusual. I asked the moms to stay and listen because I gave the girls an interesting project, and I think we should all hear what they had to say."

My mom winked at me and I got a bit more calm. Maybe this wasn't such a bad idea.

But there was still obviously the chances of me messing up, everyone laughing, a zombie apocalypse, and/or other bad scenarios.

"Their assignment was to respond to something that made them angry. Given what's been going on in our world lately, I thought we should all have a space to discuss and reflect." The mothers in the room nodded. "So Insha'Allah let's begin with Miss.....Leena Rahman!"

Leena stood at the front and opened her paper. "So the things that make me angry are probably what make others angry as well, things like soggy cereal, slow wi-fi, and buffering. But since sister Maha told us to make it meaningful, I decided to think a bit deeper."

Apparently I wasn't the only one who struggled!

Leena continued, "So I guess what makes me *really* angry is seeing innocent kids dying around the world. That's something that should make everyone angry. I think people don't realize how everybody has dreams, and everybody has hopes. Everyone deserves a chance to live."

We all clapped for her and sister Maha continued calling names. One after another girls stood up to speak, and my heart pounded inside me, almost as if it was having a boxing match with the wall of my chest.

A girl named Amira went up to the front. "I don't like

how Muslims feel like they need to change themselves in order to be accepted. We should be comfortable with who we are, no matter what, and not aim to seek some random person's approval." We all clapped.

Then Mariam talked about her little brother, which I couldn't relate to since I didn't have any siblings. But she spoke with such passion I was beginning to feel thankful I didn't have somebody to "annoy me and throw socks at my head." I guess some of us didn't go too deep.

Sister Maha called a few more girls and soon I realized I was the only one who hadn't presented yet. I felt like I was getting hot, like someone filled my insides with lava and slowly it was bubbling up and reaching my throat.

"All of you have done such an amazing job," sister Maha said. "We have one last presenter — Asal Ali, can you finish us off?"

I walked up to the front of the room and nervously hung my poster up on the wall. When I turned to face everyone I realized what a large crowd this was. I muttered *Bismillah* under my breath, took a deep breath, and began.

"So...uh how many of you have watched the series 'The Secret Life of Muslims' ?" I asked. A few girls in my group raised their hands.

"I was curious to see it, and I actually really enjoyed all the positive things it showed about being Muslim. After watching the first clip, I was feeling good." I took another deep breath. "And then I read the comments."

Some people shifted in their seats, like they clearly knew what was coming.

"It made me so upset to see so many comments that were offensive, so full of hate. And it wasn't the only time I'd seen them. So I decided that this ignorance, these cowardly attacks, were what made me truly angry. I had had enough. So..."

I waved some jazz hands over the poster board.

"This is what I did about it. I asked my friends and people in the community to write positive messages to counter the negative, like our own real life comment board. I didn't want to focus on the bad, I just wanted to emphasize the good. This board shows all the many faces of a Muslim, and I hope it can convey its own simple truth: that this is who we are, without apology. These are all the reasons we have faith, and pride, and love for each other."

I saw my mother smile at me in the crowd, and that gave me the courage to say one last thing.

"I wanted to thank everyone who opened themselves to do this project with me. And I figured I should be brave enough to be open, too, so here goes. Here's *my* sticky note:

'We Muslims have a beautiful way of life. Each rule has its own reason, and its own benefit. I am so grateful for this guidance. I am so grateful to be Muslim. I feel this deeply through the eyes of my heart: our pride will outshine any hate.'"

Applause rang out through the crowd. Not the kind that you get when you win an Oscar but still it was applause. A tingle went through my spine. I felt afloat from the inside out.

Sister Maha took center stage once again. "Masha'Allah, Asal, what a thoughtful project! Thank you for sharing and for closing us out." I beamed and blushed.

"Now, everyone," she continued, "the projects are on display, so feel free to discuss and to come take a closer look."

Sister Maha went over to help hang some other projects, and everyone got up and started milling around. My friend

Leena came and stared at my board. "Hey this is really cool!" She looked closer at one and started laughing, "This is my favorite: When everyone else is listening to Drake, I'm over here listening to Deen Squad."

"I like that one, too. Zayna wrote that," I said, grinning.

My mom walked over to give me a hug. "I'm very proud of you, Asal jaan."

"Aw you really think I did good?" I knew I did good, I just wanted to hear it from her. Is that a bad thing? Nope.

The room was buzzing with noise and conversation. It felt nice that everyone who looked at my project seemed to see something in a sticky-note they felt a connection to.

Someone asked if they could add their own sticky notes, and I said, "Sure!" And then people were lining up, waiting for their turn. I felt a sense of pride. All of these people, standing up for something I believed in, something that turned hate into love.

It wasn't a beautiful poster, certainly not fancy or artistic like the ones that make you think deep thoughts. And my words weren't perfect, nothing like the poems I read that had words that flowed together like a river, with more swimming below the surface.

But whatever art may be, this, apparently, was mine.

THE
BEAUTy
THE
of WORLd
L'Ies in the
DIVERSIty OF
Its PEOPLE

Ask me My Name

Salihah Aakil

Sometimes I wonder what I would do if I were confronted by a bigot, who hated me for what I wear and believe. I'm not sure what I would do in the moment, but right now I like to think that I would start by telling them:

"Ask me my name. Because my name is my brand and I'm sure you branded me terrorist, branded me oppressed daughter of an extremist, an extremist herself. With the hot branding iron that is your voice, you call me rag-head, jihadist, backward-thinking fool, worst thing since Black Lives Matter.

But if you asked me my name, I'd tell you that it is Salihah Amaal Aakil and this brand my mother gave me means Good-doer and Hope and Intellect. And I hope that you can use your intellect to realize that good-doers don't only look like you."

And if they still didn't get it then I'd say again:

"Ask me my name. Because is that not the first step to humanization, realizing that my mother loved me the same way yours loves you, and cared enough to give me an identity with these three simple words. Salihah Amaal Aakil, this girl standing before you asking you to understand that 'different' and 'dangerous' are not synonyms. Promising you that no matter how loud you shout, "Hey, you terrorist!" at her back, she won't respond because she's told you already that that is not her name."

And after that I'd say:

"I am not your enemy, not against, in fact this fire in my belly is made for warmth and fueled by love and yes I do love you. And no, not because anyone told me I should. Simply because you are human and although you hate me I am too. So...

Ask me my name. And I will tell you that I have many, I can't be defined by just a few syllables. My name is Broken, my name is Healing. My name is Perseverance and Prayer. Is Forgive and Move On, but not Forget, never forget, never forget the way they tried to kill you and the way you refuse to die. My name is Black and Beautiful and Muslim and Woman. My name is Salihah Amaal Aakil but my friends call me Sasa. And you, bigot standing before me now, may not."

BETW

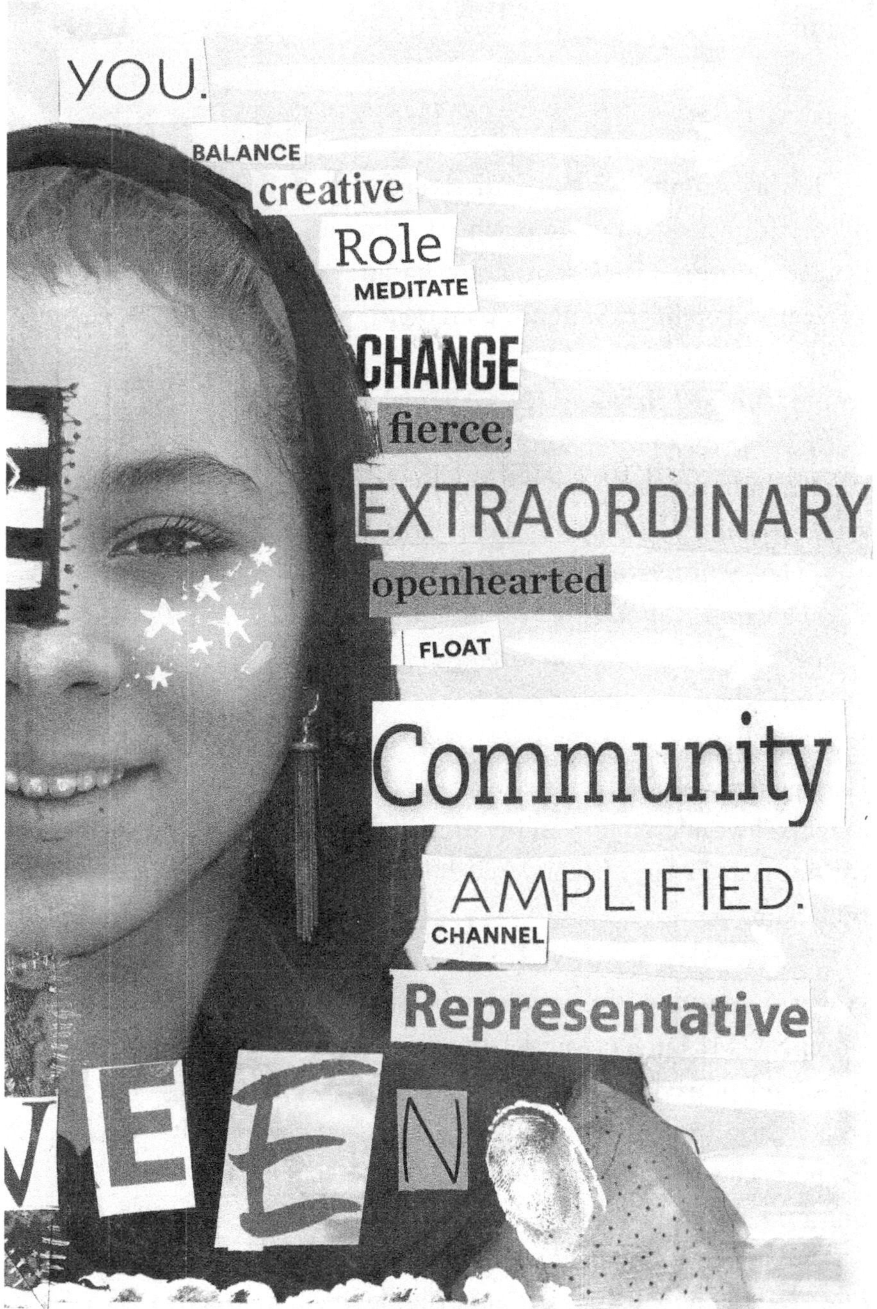
YOU.
BALANCE
creative
Role
MEDITATE
CHANGE
fierce,
EXTRAORDINARY
openhearted
FLOAT
Community
AMPLIFIED.
CHANNEL
Representative
VEEN

AFTERWORD

It was summer camp, and though the auditorium was filled with nearly a hundred school-aged children, you could hear a pin drop. They sat quietly, hanging on every word as 15-year-old camper, Salihah, confidently spoke:

> "...*This girl standing before you*
> *asking you to understand*
> *that* different *and* dangerous *are not synonyms.*
> *Promising you that no matter how loud you shout,*
> *"Hey, you terrorist!" at her back,*
> *she won't respond*
> *because she's told you already*
> *that is not her name.*"

Her spoken word left her fellow campers clearly moved, some to tears. I wondered how many of them had heard such power from a peer before; I wondered how many had experienced such pain.

Afterwards, as they stood in unison for afternoon prayer, I continued to wonder what they were thinking. As CampNWMI Director and fellow worshiper, I stood beside them and prayed as well. I prayed that the children in that congregation might be inspired to stand up confidently, too, in their schools and communities, and to speak their truths, unafraid.

All teenagers struggle to find their place in the world. For American Muslims, that struggle includes navigating multiple layers of identity as Americans, as Muslims, and as black and brown youth. The last couple years have been momentous for American Muslims. Ibtihaj Muhammad made it to the Olympics. Stores in the mall like Apple and Gap feature Muslim women in hijab. Rashida Tlaib and Ilhan Omar were elected to Congress. Yet incidents of anti-Muslim discrimination and hate crimes have risen. Hate seems to have emerged from the shadows with a new visibility, amplified through social media and forces of unrest.

While this is a challenging time, it is also a unique time filled with possibility. We at Next Wave Muslim Initiative are immensely grateful for this opportunity to let our youth's voices be heard. And we are grateful to these courageous young people for stepping up and giving us a glimpse into their world. NWMI shares in the vision of Shout Mouse Press that, through sharing stories, we see both the humanity and the diversity of the next generation of leaders. The result will be—as Salihah's words command—that we turn our backs on degradation and division, and instead, we learn each other's names.

Mona Rahnama Eldadah
Co-founder, Next Wave Muslim Initiative

ACKNOWLEDGMENTS

This book represents a collaboration between Next Wave Muslim Initiative (NWMI) and Shout Mouse Press, and we are grateful for the leadership and dedication of both teams.

For serving as the NWMI project facilitator, we thank NWMI Co-founder and Creative Director Mona Eldadah. Mona was a terrific visionary and coordinating force behind this project, and she gave selflessly of her time to make this book the best it could be. We also thank NWMI leadership, especially Mariam Mokhtarzada, who believed in the project from the beginning and encouraged us throughout.

For her overall thought leadership as well as her beautiful foreword we thank author Hena Khan. Throughout this project Hena contributed valuable insights, mentored teen writers, offered editorial feedback, and even hosted weekend workshops, complete with Pakistani brunch. Hena's support and expertise made for not only a better book, but a better community, and we are grateful.

From Shout Mouse Press, we thank "Team Story": Sarai Johnson, Zeynep Cakmak, Barrett Smith, and Eva Shapiro. Team Story mentored these writers one-on-one throughout the process of brainstorming, drafting, writing, revising, and revising again (!), and they did so with humor and with heart. Special HUGE thanks to Barrett for her essential design, editorial, and project management work; this book would not have come together without her time and talents. We are lucky to count every one of you as members of this team!

We are also enormously grateful to our Art Coach, the talented and thoughtful Sobia Ahmad. Sobia led engaging art workshops throughout the project, culminating in the striking collages featured in this book. Sobia also played an integral role in designing the cover, and she served as an essential advisor while defining the book's mission and messages. We appreciate not only Sobia's considerable artistic talents but also her deep investment in art for social justice. We are cheering her on in her own important work.

For additional graphic design support we thank Amber Colleran; her expertise helps these voices get the respect and consideration they deserve, and we are grateful. We also thank Lana Wong for her design insights, photography, and stellar proofreading, and for leading the charge to amplify these voices in the world.

None of this work would have been possible without a generous grant from the Donors InVesting in Arts Fund at the Greater Washington Community Foundation, for which we are enormously grateful. We also appreciate VisArts for providing the beautiful art and writing workshop space—especially that rooftop with the soft summer breeze.

And most of all we thank the dedicated young people of NWMI, who were moved to share not just their art and stories, but also, courageously, their truest selves. To Samaa, Noor, Imaan, Ruqayyah, Bilal, Salihah, Leyla, Fatima, Iman, and Ayah: it's been an honor, and a joy. Thank you for the many laughs, and the many lessons. We are so proud of you, and we believe in your ability to foster peace, understanding, connection, and grace. We need you. Thank you. We cannot wait to see what you will do next.

Kathy Crutcher
Founder, Shout Mouse Press

ABOUT THE AUTHORS

AYAH NOOR

My name is Ayah Noor. Ayah means 'sign from God' or 'miracle,' and Noor means 'light.' From my mother's side I am Afghan, and from my father's side I'm American.

I am 14 years old. My mom has been homeschooling me since the day I was born and I love it too much to ever stop. There is an ever-growing list of things I am interested in, including art, dancing, Spider-Man, anatomy, cats, ancient artifacts, antiques, learning languages, and tea.

I have never wanted to fit in. I have no interest in changing who I am in order to be liked. I don't want to twist my values or bend my faith or be Muslim in a way that others find acceptable. I don't want to do that. I don't need to prove anything.

I simply want to be respected, and to not have to live with rude stares, or fear. I ask this not because I am special, but simply because of what unifies everyone. When you take away race, religion, ethnicity, color, and fandoms, you are left with a human. Each with their own story, but all in the same world.

BILAL SALEEM

My name's Bilal. I play the guitar. I listen to rap music. I'm a Muslim. I'm currently writing this as a high school senior, but by the time this is published, I will (most likely) have graduated. I'm undecided when it comes to what I'm trying to do in college, but I'm cool with that. Before applying to be part of this project, I didn't really write much. Like, I could write, but I didn't. It was my mother, Hena Khan, also an author, that got the gears rolling, and got me to make an effort.

I'm really blessed, getting to grow up in Rockville, MD. It's an extremely diverse and accepting community that's never really made me feel out of place or unheard. I guess that's why I felt obligated to write, because I know not everyone has that experience. It was cool to have this opportunity to make my voice heard, and to help others understand that just because I'm a Muslim doesn't make me very different.

You'll see throughout my piece that it's less about my life as a Muslim, and more about how Islam seeps into being a regular American teen. You'll see I chose to write about music, something universal that people can connect to. You'll see that I'm just an extraordinarily ordinary kid, and I hope you enjoy my musings.

SAMAA ELDADAH

I'm a senior at Sandy Spring Friends School in Sandy Spring, MD. High school has taught me a lot about the power of youth voices, and one of my immediate goals is to translate the organizing I've done in school into programming for my Muslim peers. My long-term goals include college, potentially law school, and making a local political impact.

I'm also a second-generation Middle Eastern American. My mom's side of the family is from Iran, and my dad's side is from Iraq. My grandparents on both sides have offered me glimpses into worlds completely different from my own–worlds that are often painted in negative lights by Western media.

For me, the NWMI x Shout Mouse collaboration was a celebration of nuanced identities. I've always been the only hijabi in my school and, as a result, I've been the de facto representative of all things Muslim for my non-Muslim peers. I've felt pressure—often self-imposed—to be more "American" or more "Muslim." Recently, I've realized that it's OK to be both without compromise. My hope is that this book can be an homage, not just to the American Muslim teen experience, but to the experience of all minority American kids as we navigate the world at the intersection of our identities.

Salihah Aakil

My name is Salihah "Sasa" Aakil. I'm a sophomore in high school in Silver Spring, Maryland. I enjoy writing, painting, doing pottery, and talking to people. I like hunting down stories, asking people about their experiences, and creating art after them: sometimes for healing, sometimes for remembering, sometimes for rebellion.

I am a Black American Muslim Woman—my family has been in America since slave ships and before. On my father's side I'm African-American and American-Indian, and on my mother's side I am Panamanian and African-American. I'm a third-generation Muslim, Writer, and Artist. I wrote this series of poems and vignettes because I wanted to share my story. Not for proof or justification or validation, just because that's what stories are for—sharing. I've never been rich in anything but stories, and if one of them happens to change someone's ideas, open their heart, give them joy, or show them that they can do what I do and better, then Alhamdulillah. Maybe they'll end up rich like I am.

Imaan Shanavas

I am a junior at Poolesville High School, where I serve as the president of the Muslim Student Association. Through this organization, we hold food drives and food packaging for the poor. We also coordinate discussions where Muslims and non-Muslims can have a safe space to discuss Islam and address misconceptions.

In the future, I plan to attend college and hopefully go to dental school. I enjoy Netflix, napping, and eating basically anything.

My mother is from Pakistan, while my dad is from India. However, they both grew up in the U.S. Growing up in Montgomery County, Maryland, one of the most diverse counties in the United States, I rarely encountered prejudice. However, after the political scene began to change, the Syrian refugee crisis showed me how fear of unknown cultures can cause misunderstanding, discrimination, and disregard for human life. It hurt me that so many people feared Syrian families who were simply trying to find a safe home. This is why I joined this project—so that we as Muslims can share our diverse views and common human values, to shrink that distance between all of us and the unknown.

IMAN ILIAS

My name is Iman Ilias. I'm a freshman at Walt Whitman High School in Bethesda, Maryland. I am a second-generation Pakistani Muslim American. I'm a biryani-and-popcorn-holic :-)

I've been so honored and grateful to be a part of this project, because the fact of the matter is that Muslim Americans don't often have a chance to show who they really are and what they really want. For me, this project wasn't about discrimination, or civil rights, or even minority representation. This project was about a group of bright minds from different backgrounds and different outlooks coming together to show what their lives are truly like. What I hope people get out of my piece is that it's okay to be more than one thing. It's perfectly fine, and enriching, in fact, to have a hyphenated identity. Being Muslim and a normal American teenager aren't mutually exclusive, but then again, neither are any other two identities. I wrote this for anyone who's ever felt different, and who needs to be reminded that that's a beautiful thing.

Leyla Rasheed

My name is Leyla Rasheed, and I am a freshman at the Holton-Arms School in Bethesda, MD. I enjoy playing soccer, biking, writing, and ceramics. I am an active member of the Islamic Community Center of Potomac.

As the only Muslim in my primarily white freshman class, it can be hard to step up or stand out, for fear that my actions may be used to generalize all other Muslims. Joining this book project with NWMI and Shout Mouse has really helped me to activate my voice as a young American Muslim. Sharing my story is my own small way of defying the stereotypes I face everyday. I hope that my writing inspires anyone trying to find their own voice, and that it helps start conversations that are much overdue.

Noor Saleem

My name is Noor Saleem. I'm a junior at National Cathedral School in Washington, DC, and during my free time I enjoy writing poetry, playing soccer, and relaxing to music.

I am a Muslim Arab-American. I was born in the United States, the second-generation daughter of two Muslim-Iraqi parents. Some of my peers might tell me that I don't "look Arab," but I speak Arabic fluently at home, have grown up surrounded by the influence of Arab culture, and live my life grounded by the values of my faith.

I know many others my age who talk about their identity with varying degrees of discomfort, but our generation of youth cannot afford that luxury when dealing with prejudice. The ideals that this country was built on, ones of equality, justice, and representation, are crumbling under a discriminatory narrative. I care about speaking up and putting forward my personal narrative because something has to change, and change has never originated from passivity.

ABOUT THE ARTISTS

Ruqayyah Aakil

Collage Artist

Photographer

My name is Ruqayyah Aakil. I am a homeschooled senior in Silver Spring, Maryland. I enjoy photography, puzzles, binge-watching TV shows, and music. I like going outdoors—not to go hiking or anything like that—but just to breathe the fresh air and take in the world, whether it is through my eyes or the viewfinder of a camera.

I am a Black American Muslim. On my dad's side I am African-American and American Indian, and on my mom's side I am African-American and Panamanian. I am a third-generation Muslim, an artist, and a future engineer.

My family was always different wherever we went. We looked different. But yet, in some way, we also always had something in common with the people we were around. I decided to take part in this project not only to show the world my art, but also to let the world know that even though we are different, we still have similarities. We have similarities, not only through many shared beliefs, but also because growing up in this country, everyone struggles. We are exactly the same from that standpoint. We all have struggles no matter what our race, religion, or gender. And that's part of why I joined this project.

FATIMA RAFIE

COLLAGE ARTIST
ILLUSTRATOR OF *KABOB SQUAD*

I'm currently a junior at Oakton High school in Vienna, Virginia. I like many different things, like drawing, taekwondo, graphic design, math, chemistry, psychology, reading... The list goes on. Basically, I try to keep myself occupied with learning as many new skills as I can, so that I make the most of the time I have as a teenager.

I am the first of my family to have been born in the U.S. Both of my parents are from Iran, and I am the first of their four children. Despite our physical detachment from Iran, my siblings and I have been able to learn a lot about our culture and traditions, in some cases even more than about American culture. In fact, my first sister and I didn't even speak English until we started pre-school.

But there was one thing that set our family apart the most from our American neighbors: Islam. My whole life I've heard the West say negative things about my faith, but in my experience, it has taught me nothing but how to live a peaceful and humble life. I want to do exactly that. For this reason, I decided to join the NWMI x Shout Mouse team—to dispel negative perceptions of Islam that have been fueled by fear and ignorance. And to let it be known that Islam is neither a race nor an ethnicity, it is a religion, a way of life that welcomes all who wish to experience it, regardless of their background.

SHOUT MOUSE PRESS

Shout Mouse Press is a nonprofit writing and publishing program dedicated to amplifying unheard voices. Through writing workshops that lead to professional publication, we empower writers from marginalized backgrounds to tell their own stories in their own voices and—as published authors—to act as agents of change.

In partnership with other nonprofits serving communities in need, we are building a catalog of mission-driven books by unheard voices. Our authors have produced original children's books, comics, novels, and memoir and poetry collections that expand empathy, advance social justice, and increase understanding of unheard perspectives.

Learn more at shoutmousepress.org.

NEXT WAVE MUSLIM INITIATIVE

Next Wave Muslim Initiative (NWMI) is a nonprofit organization founded in 2009, dedicated to serving the American Muslim community of the Washington metropolitan area by promoting Islamic principles—such as self-development, community service, and social justice—through meaningful programming and projects.

Learn more at nwmi.org.

ALSO BY SHOUT MOUSE PRESS

Voces Sin Fronteras (2018), Latin American Youth Center.
Immigrant youth tell true life stories through comics and essays in this bilingual graphic memoir collection.

The Day Tajon Got Shot (2017), Beacon House.
Teen authors explore a police shooting from multiple perspectives in this collaborative novel.

The Untold Story of The Real Me: Young Voices From Prison (2016), Free Minds Book Club & Writing Workshop.
Incarcerated youth share raw and powerful poetry, with profiles and portraits of returned citizens.

How to Grow Up Like Me (2014), Our Lives Matter (2015), Humans of Ballou (2016),The Ballou We Know (2019).
Students from Ballou High School in Washington, DC speak for themselves through photos and essays.

For the full catalog of #OwnVoices teen-authored Shout Mouse Press books, including illustrated children's books, visit shoutmousepress.org.

Books are also available through Amazon, select bookstores, and select distributors, including Ingram and Follett.

For bulk orders, educator inquiries, and nonprofit discounts contact orders@shoutmousepress.org.

WE BELIEVE

We believe everyone has a story to tell. We believe everyone has the ability to tell it. We believe by listening to the stories we tell each other—whether true or imagined, of hopes or heartbreaks or fantasies or fears—we are learning empathy, diplomacy, reflection, and grace. We believe we need to see ourselves in the stories we are surrounded by. We believe this is especially true for those who are made to believe that their stories do not matter: the poor or the sick or the marginalized or the battered. We feel lucky to be able to help unearth these stories, and we are passionate about sharing these unheard voices with the world.

Made in the USA
Middletown, DE
12 August 2020